Contents

ASHE Higher Education Report: Volume 43, Number 1
Kelly Ward, Lisa E. Wolf-Wendel, Series Editors

Mentoring Undergraduate Students

Gloria Crisp, Vicki L. Baker, Kimberly A. Griffin,
Laura Gail Lunsford, and Meghan J. Pifer

Mentoring Undergraduate Students
Gloria Crisp, Vicki L. Baker, Kimberly A. Griffin, Laura Gail Lunsford, and Meghan J. Pifer
ASHE Higher Education Report: Volume 43, Number 1
Series Editors: Kelly Ward, Lisa E. Wolf-Wendel

ASHE HIGHER EDUCATION REPORT, (Print ISSN: 1551-6970; Online ISSN: 1554-6306), is published quarterly by Wiley Subscrip
Services, Inc., a Wiley Company, 111 River St., Hoboken, NJ 07030-5774 USA.
Postmaster: Send all address changes to *ASHE HIGHER EDUCATION REPORT*, John Wiley & Sons Inc., C/O The Sheridan Press, PO Box
Hanover, PA 17331 USA.

Information for subscribers
ASHE HIGHER EDUCATION REPORT is published in 6 issues per year. Institutional subscription prices for 2017 are:
Print & Online: US$477 (US), US$557 (Canada & Mexico), US$626 (Rest of World), €406 (Europe), £323 (UK). Prices are exclusive of tax.
Pacific GST, Canadian GST/HST and European VAT will be applied at the appropriate rates. For more information on current tax rates, pleas
to www.wileyonlinelibrary.com/tax-vat. The price includes online access to the current and all online back-files to January 1st 2013, where avail
For other pricing options, including access information and terms and conditions, please visit www.wileyonlinelibrary.com/access.

Delivery Terms and Legal Title
Where the subscription price includes print issues and delivery is to the recipient's address, delivery terms are **Delivered at Place (DAP)**; the reci
is responsible for paying any import duty or taxes. Title to all issues transfers FOB our shipping point, freight prepaid. We will endeavor to f
claims for missing or damaged copies within six months of publication, within our reasonable discretion and subject to availability.

Back issues: Single issues from current and recent volumes are available at the current single issue price from cs-journals@wiley.com.

Disclaimer
The Publisher and Editors cannot be held responsible for errors or any consequences arising from the use of information contained in this journal
views and opinions expressed do not necessarily reflect those of the Publisher and Editors, neither does the publication of advertisements const
any endorsement by the Publisher and Editors of the products advertised.

Publisher: ASHE HIGHER EDUCATION REPORT is published by Wiley Periodicals, Inc., 350 Main St., Malden, MA 02148-5020.

Journal Customer Services: For ordering information, claims and any enquiry concerning your journal subscription please ge
www.wileycustomerhelp.com/ask or contact your nearest office.
Americas: Email: cs-journals@wiley.com; Tel: +1 781 388 8598 or +1 800 835 6770 (toll free in the USA & Canada).
Europe, Middle East and Africa: Email: cs-journals@wiley.com; Tel: +44 (0) 1865 778315.
Asia Pacific: Email: cs-journals@wiley.com; Tel: +65 6511 8000.
Japan: For Japanese speaking support, Email: cs-japan@wiley.com.
Visit our Online Customer Help available in 7 languages at www.wileycustomerhelp.com/ask

Production Editor: Poornita Jugran (email: pjugran@wiley.com).

Wiley's Corporate Citizenship initiative seeks to address the environmental, social, economic, and ethical challenges faced in our business and w
are important to our diverse stakeholder groups. Since launching the initiative, we have focused on sharing our content with those in need, enhan
community philanthropy, reducing our carbon impact, creating global guidelines and best practices for paper use, establishing a vendor code of e
and engaging our colleagues and other stakeholders in our efforts. Follow our progress at www.wiley.com/go/citizenship

View this journal online at wileyonlinelibrary.com/journal/aehe

Wiley is a founding member of the UN-backed HINARI, AGORA, and OARE initiatives. They are now collectively known as Research4Life, ma
online scientific content available free or at nominal cost to researchers in developing countries. Please visit Wiley's Content Access - Corp
Citizenship site: http://www.wiley.com/WileyCDA/Section/id-390082.html

Printed in the USA by The Sheridan Group.

Address for Editorial Correspondence: Coeditors-in -chief, Kelly Ward, Lisa E. Wolf-Wendel, ASHE HIGHER EDUCATION REPORT, E
lwolf@ku.edu and kaward@wsu.edu

Abstracting and Indexing Services
The Journal is indexed by Academic Search Alumni Edition (EBSCO Publishing); Education Index/Abstracts (EBSCO Publishing); ERIC: E
tional Resources Information Center (CSC); Higher Education Abstracts (Claremont Graduate University); IBR & IBZ: International Bibliogra
of Periodical Literature (KG Saur).

Cover design: Wiley
Cover Images: ©

For submission instructions, subscription and all other information visit:
wileyonlinelibrary.com/journal/aehe

Executive Summary

PROVIDING COLLEGE STUDENTS with access to mentoring has become a national priority, as evidenced by the prevalence and diversity of formal and informal mentoring programs and practices at postsecondary institutions. Mentoring efforts can be effective in addressing key issues and problems currently facing colleges and universities across the country, including the need to increase degree completion rates, reduce inequities in outcomes for marginalized and underrepresented groups, and broaden participation in the science, technology, engineering, and math (STEM) pipeline and workforce. Mentoring has long been considered a developmental and retention strategy for undergraduate students, and research suggests mentoring efforts are positively related to a variety of developmental and academic outcomes.

Unfortunately, mentoring research has been repeatedly observed by scholars to be underdeveloped relative to the importance and growing number of mentoring programs supported at the national, state, and local levels. Robust research is needed to guide the development, implementation, and assessment of undergraduate mentoring efforts. As the number of studies focused on mentoring undergraduate students continues to grow, comprehensive reviews of the literature are necessary to synthesize new knowledge. Literature reviews provide an efficient and robust way for practitioners and researchers to make sense of a large body of literature and to identify evidence-based practices specific to designing, implementing, and evaluating mentoring programs.

The most recent comprehensive review of the mentoring literature was conducted by Crisp and Cruz (2009), who provided a critical synthesis of empirical research conducted between 1990 and 2007. Although findings pointed to the overall effectiveness of mentoring as a means to develop undergraduate students and support their academic success, the review also identified persistent conceptual, methodological, and theoretical weaknesses that impede the usefulness of findings in guiding the development of mentoring practice. Fortunately, the mentoring literature appears to have evolved substantially over the past decade, with over 100 studies published on mentoring undergraduate students since the last systematic review. However, it is unclear if or how the previously discussed limitations have been addressed by mentoring scholars or to what degree knowledge has developed in recent years. Renewed consideration of knowledge, and remaining unanswered questions, about mentoring undergraduate students is thus warranted.

The overarching purpose of this monograph is to move the mentoring conversation forward by offering an updated synthesis of the undergraduate mentoring scholarship published between 2008 and 2015. We sought to address four specific questions. First, we wanted to identify and understand how empirical knowledge and theory have advanced since the last comprehensive review. Importantly, we find that recent scholarship provides a more complex understanding of how mentoring can promote social justice and equity in higher education by providing more focus to student groups that have been historically understudied and underserved in higher education. We also find that the reviewed research has provided more attention to theory, as well as practical matters such as what mentoring looks like and how it is perceived and experienced by undergraduate students. Further, our review synthesizes current understanding of mentor matching processes and activities that mentors engage in with students, which are expected to be of use in guiding the development and implementation of mentoring programs.

At the same time, findings highlight enduring conceptual, theoretical, and methodological limitations of the usefulness of research in guiding mentoring practice. One such limitation is ambiguity in how mentoring has been defined and conceptualized across studies. In response, a second goal of the monograph was to identify and provide clarity about the characteristics that serve to meaningfully distinguish mentoring relationships and programmatic efforts. Consistent with prior reviews, no one definition was found to accurately represent the diversity of relationships that students and institutional agents may term "mentoring." Rather, findings suggest that definitions of mentoring might be improved by describing the characteristics that distinguish mentoring relationships and programs. In particular, we suggest that undergraduate mentoring relationships may be differentiated by the following characteristics: (a) relationship features, (b) form or source of the relationship, (c) relationship structure, (d) program types, and (e) forms of mentoring support provided to the student. In terms of formal programmatic efforts, this monograph details four distinct, and yet in some ways overlapping, types of mentoring programs. These include orientation and university retention programs, mentoring for social justice and equity, peer mentoring, and undergraduate research and honors programs.

Another enduring limitation of the mentoring literature is the underdevelopment and relative absence of theory available to guide the administration of mentoring programs. Although there are a fair number of theories that aim to identify and define the components of mentoring relationships, scholarship that sheds light on how mentoring is related to student development, learning, and success was shown to be particularly limited. Those applying theoretical or conceptual frameworks often develop models specific to their individual research, borrowed from or based on frameworks designed to explain relationships in business. Theoretical models that continue to interrogate how identity can shape how mentoring is defined, how individuals engage one another, and the needs of protégés are important for advancing mentoring research and practice.

As such, the third goal in developing this monograph was to integrate theory and research in a way that could provide tentative hypotheses regarding the relationship between the various characteristics and outcomes of mentoring. We draw upon reviewed theory and empirical findings to offer an integrated conceptual framework that identifies connections between developmental relationships, students' characteristics, educational contexts, relationship features such as intent and intensity, forms of support, and potential short- and long-term effects on students' college experiences and outcomes. Among other things, our framework acknowledges the interconnectedness between students and their educational context. Students choose and influence their educational environments, and environments simultaneously act upon and shape students, driving their needs and resources. Additionally, our model offers testable ideas regarding how mentoring activities indirectly and directly can have an impact on intermediate and long-term student outcomes.

An important and yet often overlooked responsibility of scholars is to effectively bridge research and practice. With that in mind, our fourth and final goal in developing this monograph was to offer evidence-based practices for the administration of formal mentoring programs. Although there are a growing number of online resources to guide practitioners in developing undergraduate mentoring programs, we find that few are firmly grounded in theory and/or rigorous empirical evidence specific to undergraduate students. As such, our monograph concludes with a set of specific recommendations and evidence-based practices expected to be useful in designing, implementing, and evaluating mentoring efforts in undergraduate education.

Foreword

M ENTORING IS OFTEN looked to by faculty and administrators as a means to integrate and connect undergraduate students with the academic experience. Mentors play a clear role in student success. In *Mentoring Undergraduate Students*, authors Gloria Crisp, Vicki Baker, Kimberly Griffin, Laura Gail Lunsford, and Meghan Pifer do a great job of analyzing and synthesizing current literature related to all aspects of undergraduate mentoring from definition to theory to practice to informing ongoing research. The compendium of research reviewed provides practitioners and researchers with an evidence-based view of the influence of mentoring on the academic and social integration of undergraduate students.

Mentoring is one of those concepts in higher education that few disagree is a "good" thing for students and faculty. What is often missing, however, is how mentoring actually influences and shapes the student experience. Does mentoring help retention? How does mentoring contribute to learning and development? What types of mentoring programs assist students from diverse backgrounds? When it comes time to fund programs or start new projects or maintain programs after a grant, it is useful to have evidence of a particular practice to help address these and other questions. In this monograph, the authors provide information about different kinds of mentoring, examples of best practice, and evidence of impact of different kinds of mentoring.

The monograph is sure to be of interest to those who study mentoring and other aspects of student success. In addition, the monograph is a great tool for those who work with undergraduate students to initiate and maintain mentoring programs. Those involved in assessment of student learning and outcomes will also find the monograph a valuable resource because it provides a framework to show how mentoring influences the student experience and student learning and development outcomes.

The contents of the monograph are comprehensive and go beyond description. The authors provide an analysis of the literature and include discussion of the role that mentoring can play in integrating students from historically underrepresented groups in higher education and also address the role that mentoring can play in advancing social justice and equity agendas. Many faculty and student affairs practitioners in higher education know of the merits of mentoring for supporting students from underrepresented minority groups in higher education, and the authors of the monograph review related literature and highlight programs that can provide ideas for transferable practice.

The treatment of the topic of mentoring in the monograph is helpful as well given the focus on the administration of mentoring programs. The authors address literature about how to develop and implement programs and the nuances of making mentor matches. Further, the authors address the importance of context and how mentoring programs are shaped by different types of missions for programs (e.g., for athletes, honors programs, first-generation students). Not all mentoring programs or approaches are the same. Different contexts call for different approaches and the authors address and include literature related to such distinctions.

Readers will find this monograph a helpful tool to understand the nuances of different types of mentoring programs (e.g., peer mentoring), theoretical and conceptual models related to mentoring, and further thinking about who is doing the mentoring and who is mentored. Further, those who study concepts related to mentoring will find this monograph an incredibly helpful tool to help frame and conceptualize future research. In my own reading of this monograph, it was great to have a review of concepts related to mentoring that are often taken for granted in both research and practice. I applaud the authors for providing a solid literature base to inform ongoing research and practice. I learned from reading this monograph and I hope you, as a reader, will as well.

Kelly Ward
Series Editor

Introduction

MENTORING HAS BECOME a national priority in recent years. Mentorship is a key component of the White House initiative, My Brother's Keeper, focused on the success and development of African American boys and men. MENTOR: The National Mentoring Partnership published *The Mentoring Effect* in 2014, which called for a national commitment to mentoring given its positive influence on decision making, aspirations, and outcomes of youth in the United States (Bruce & Bridgeland, 2014). Mentoring efforts have also been recommended as a central strategy in addressing key issues and problems currently facing colleges and universities across the country. For example, mentoring initiatives contribute to the Completion Agenda, a national movement led largely by policymakers to increase college completion rates through improved policies and practices.

Mentoring has long been considered a developmental and retention strategy for undergraduate education (Jacobi, 1991) and research suggests mentoring relationships are positively related to a variety of academic outcomes such as persistence and grades (e.g., Collings, Swanson, & Watkins, 2014; Khazanov, 2011). It is important to note that mentoring efforts have also been found to support social justice by providing equitable forms and types of support (and subsequent equitable outcomes) for underrepresented and underserved groups such as African American, Latina/o, and low-income students (e.g., Dahlvig, 2010; Tovar, 2014). Furthermore, there is growing evidence that mentoring programs may be an effective means to diversify the science, technology, engineering, and math (STEM) pipeline and workforce (e.g.,

Slovacek et al., 2011), with such practices growing beyond STEM fields to other professional fields such as business (Baker, 2016).

Despite its importance in providing greater access to key relationships, research about mentoring relationships has been repeatedly critiqued and observed by scholars as underdeveloped (e.g., Crisp & Cruz, 2009; Jacobi, 1991). Although the literature base has been growing steadily over the past few decades, mentoring research and theory continue to lag behind program development and implementation efforts at the local, state, and national levels. Rigorous mentoring research is needed to guide the formation of program development and implementation and to evaluate program effectiveness. Additionally, comprehensive reviews of the literature are necessary to make sense of and synthesize the growing number of research studies focused on mentoring undergraduate students. Literature reviews can be a useful tool to both researchers and practitioners by providing a synthesis of current findings, which acknowledge and account for new streams of research within broad categories (e.g., social justice and equity). Such reviews are also valuable for developing high-quality programs and providing evidence-based practices for local, state, and national mentoring efforts. For instance, reviews can help to identify measures of quality including the frequency and consistency of interaction, feelings of connection between the mentor and protégé, and mentors' and protégés' approaches to the relationship. Taken together, these measures help to create a more holistic picture of mentoring relationships by serving as a model of how to manage such relationships from both the mentor and protégé perspectives and providing insights into what makes a mentorship a successful relationship.

Although scholarship focused on mentoring undergraduate students has continued to expand in recent years, particularly over the past decade, there has not been a comprehensive review of the mentoring literature since Crisp and Cruz's (2009) review of empirical work conducted between 1990 and 2007. The present monograph provides an updated comprehensive review of mentoring research published between 2008 and 2015. This first chapter provides an introduction to mentoring, including more explanation regarding why mentoring undergraduate students is important and how such efforts serve to address enduring issues and concerns surrounding postsecondary institutions, such as social justice and degree completion. A review of mentoring definitions is offered, followed by a more detailed discussion of the characteristics that distinguish mentoring from other relationships. A summary of findings from relevant and recent literature reviews follows, before the purpose of the monograph and guiding questions are presented.

Importance and Value of Mentoring

In 2015, over 90% of 25- to 29-year-olds living in the United States had completed high school, with 44% of these individuals holding an associate's degree and only 34% having earned a bachelor's degree or higher (Kena et al., 2016). The broader line of student success research has repeatedly observed the importance of faculty–student interactions and mentorship to undergraduate students' academic progress and success (Museus & Neville, 2012; Pascarella & Terenzini, 2005). Additionally, colleges and universities that actively foster such interactions are likely to realize benefits at the institutional (e.g., retention rates) and individual (e.g., degree attainment) levels (Komarraju, Musulkin, & Bhattacharya, 2010).

Mentoring programs and associated efforts can be effective means of supporting student development and academic success. Some notable outcomes of mentoring undergraduate students include increased academic performance as measured on exam scores and in grade point averages (GPAs), and involvement in program-related activities (Brittian, Sy, & Stokes, 2009; Dahlvig, 2010). Longer term academic success outcomes related to mentoring include greater degree attainment and persistence (Espinoza & Espinoza, 2012; Gross, Iverson, Willett, & Manduca, 2015). Further, mentoring has been positively linked to developmental outcomes that contribute to academic success including college adjustment (Smojver Ažić & Antulic, 2013), career and personal development (Kinkel, 2011), and civic outcomes such as social responsibility and socially responsive leadership (Haddock et al., 2013).

Mentoring also has a great deal of potential to promote social justice by supporting and equalizing academic outcomes for traditionally marginalized and underrepresented students. Mentoring is something every undergraduate student needs, yet students from working-class backgrounds (Dunstan & Jaeger, 2015); first-generation students (Parks-Yancy, 2012); African American, Latina/o, and American Indian/Native students (Rios-Aguilar & Deil-Amen, 2010; Tovar, 2014); and others from historically underrepresented groups may not have equitable access to mentoring support when compared to majority groups.

Further, these students may not bring the same types of resources to college compared to their majority-group peers (Museus & Neville, 2012). The first year of college can be challenging, particularly for those students who are the first in their families to attend college and/or are from underserved groups (Owens, Lacey, Rawls, & Holbert-Quince, 2010; Phinney, Campos, Cidhinnia, Padilla Kallemeyn, & Kim, 2011). Mentoring has the potential to support national and institutional goals to increase the number of persons completing college degrees by providing access to social capital—opportunities and resources provided through relationships and interpersonal networks (Palmer & Gasman, 2008)—and cultural capital, or social assets that promote mobility (Cole & Espinoza, 2008). Through mentoring programs, students participate in activities aimed at development in areas such as study skills, time management, and written and oral communication skills (Michael, Dickson, Ryan, & Koefer, 2010; Salinitri, 2005), providing opportunities to identify ways of successfully navigating the college environment. Students from underrepresented groups may also have fewer peers and role models who share their identity characteristics and related experiences and may be competing for the limited number of such supporters. Students also may benefit from peer mentoring and other social support in the cohort experience built into many mentoring programs aimed at college adjustment.

Mentoring also directly addresses the need to diversify the STEM disciplines, which have historically not included underrepresented minority students (Perna et al., 2009), and is one of the most prominent efforts to increase the number of individuals from underrepresented groups earning degrees in STEM fields (Behar-Horenstein, Roberts, & Dix, 2010). Supportive mentoring relationships have the potential to increase career ambition and awareness (Parks-Yancy, 2012) and aid students' professional identity development (Murdock, Stipanovic, & Lucas, 2013). Although the design and structure of programs vary, STEM-related mentoring efforts can be effective in engaging students in research with graduate students and faculty who serve as mentors in guiding and supporting students' career aspirations and sense of belonging on campus generally and in STEM programs specifically.

Mentoring Definitions and Characteristics

There is no one definition that accurately represents the diversity of relationships that students and institutional agents may term "mentoring." The absence of a widely accepted definition of mentoring is well documented (see Jacobi, 1991; Johnson, 1989; Miller, 2002). For instance, a literature review by Crisp and Cruz (2009) identified over 50 definitions of mentoring varying in scope and breadth. Published mentoring studies, program websites, and other associated documentation may intentionally or unintentionally exclude a definition of mentoring (Crisp & Cruz, 2009). Kram (1985) offered a foundational definition often used by scholars, describing mentoring as a relationship between two individuals whereby the more experienced person is committed to providing developmental support to the other, less experienced person.

Other definitions of mentoring are broader, and may apply to relationships across learning and educational contexts (e.g., Johnson, 2003; Ragins & McFarlin, 1990). Mentoring has been frequently described as a concept or process as well as a set of developmental activities performed by an individual termed "mentor." For instance, Blackwell (1989) defined mentoring as a "process by which persons of a superior rank, special achievements, and prestige instruct, counsel, guide, and facilitate the intellectual and/or career development of persons identified as protégés" (p. 9). In other cases, the definition of mentoring is framed around the types of support that are provided to the student by a mentor. Jacobi (1991) described mentors as individuals who provide emotional and psychological support, career advice, and role modeling in a relationship that is often mutually beneficial.

Further, it is not uncommon for the definition of mentoring to be bound to a particular mentoring program. Jacobi (1991) noted that mentoring programs are often so diverse that they actually may have little in common. For example, Goff (2011) defined mentoring within the context of a peer mentoring experience that pairs two or more students with the more experienced student taking on a mentoring role and providing instruction, support, and guidance to the less experienced student or group. In contrast, Craney, McKay, Mazzeo, and Morris (2011) describe mentoring as students and faculty members working together to develop and implement a research proposal.

Although definitions of mentoring may be expected to vary across studies and programs, there appear to be at least four points of consensus across studies (Crisp & Cruz, 2009; Jacobi, 1991):

1. Mentoring relationships are focused on the growth and development of students and can be constructed in various forms.
2. Mentoring experiences may include broad forms of support that include professional, career, and emotional support.
3. Mentoring relationships are personal and reciprocal.
4. Relative to their students, mentors have more experience, influence, or achievement within the educational environment.

In addition to the points discussed here, definitions of mentoring may be better understood by describing the characteristics that serve to bound and distinguish mentoring relationships and programs. Mentoring characteristics include (a) relationship features, (b) form or source of the relationship, (c) relationship structure, (d) program types, and (e) forms of mentoring support. Note that each of these characteristics is discussed in more detail throughout the monograph, as they serve as the foundation for the conceptual model presented in the fifth chapter.

Mentoring relationships can be characterized by several features including the intent, purpose, intensity, and duration of the relationship. In short, mentoring involves a purposeful and intentional commitment on the part of the mentor to the growth, development, and success of the student, which is rooted in long-term caring (Baker & Griffin, 2010). Mentoring relationships may also be characterized by the forms or sources of "mentors" including faculty members, staff members (e.g., academic advisor), graduate students, and peers.

As is discussed in the next section, it is important to recognize that each of these forms or sources of support can—and often do—provide different and unique forms of mentoring support to students. Mentoring relationships are bound by the structure of the relationship. Although the most common mentoring structure involves a one-on-one, face-to-face relationship between mentor and student, mentoring relationships may also be structured to include multiple students, otherwise known as group mentoring. It is also increasingly common for mentoring relationships to connect via technology, commonly referred to as e-mentoring. Further, we would be remiss if we did not acknowledge the prevalence of natural mentoring relationships that develop organically between students and mentors and function outside of a formal mentoring program.

It is becoming increasingly common for mentoring relationships to be studied and understood within the context of broader programmatic efforts designed to support student success, including orientation and first-year experience programs, mentoring programs focused on promoting social justice, peer mentoring programs, and undergraduate research and honors programs that include a mentoring component. As discussed in the third chapter, orientation programs support transition into college and help students develop academic and social skills as well as support persistence, retention, and overall engagement in the academic and campus communities. Mentoring programs targeted toward underrepresented populations also seek to support students in degree completion and perhaps advanced study, particularly in fields in which underrepresented populations are underenrolled such as in STEM. Much like orientation programs, the goal is to support persistence, retention, and engagement as well as promote social justice by reducing inequities in participation and outcomes for underserved groups. Research and honors programs are typically focused on a disciplinary domain and serve as an opportunity to help students develop their research skills and engage in the research process. As part of their participation, undergraduate students may write a thesis, engage in an independent study, or support a faculty member on her or his research project. Such experiences contribute to GPA and increased

TABLE 1
Characteristics of Mentoring Relationships

Characteristic	Description/Examples
Relationship Features	intent, purpose, intensity, duration
Form of Relationship	faculty, staff, graduate students, peers
Relationship Structure	individual one on one, group, e-mentoring, natural relationships
Program Types	orientation and retention, mentoring programs designed to support targeted populations, peer mentoring programs, undergraduate research and honors programs
Forms of Support	psychological and emotional support, degree support, career support, academic subject knowledge support

self-efficacy. Finally, peer mentoring is both a type of mentoring program and also an important source of support that may be provided within other types of mentoring programs.

Describing the forms of mentoring support offered within mentoring relationships provide another meaningful way to understand mentoring relationships. In her foundational mentoring work, Kram (1985, 1988) identified two broad forms of support that mentoring relationships can and should provide: career support and psychosocial support. Jacobi (1991) considered these two forms of support, along with an additional form of support that she termed role modeling (e.g., having someone to look up to and emulate their behavior). Recent theoretical and empirical work by Crisp and colleagues (Crisp 2009, 2010; Crisp & Cruz, 2009, 2010; Nora & Crisp, 2007) extended Kram's and Jacobi's frameworks to suggest that mentoring undergraduate students involves four forms of support, including psychological and emotional support, degree and career support, academic subject knowledge support, and the existence of a role model. The characteristics of mentoring are summarized in Table 1.

The following vignette illustrates how these characteristics of mentoring may come together in practice:

Maria is a senior at Rural College working on her honors thesis in psychology. She hopes to pursue graduate studies and works closely with Professor Smith, her thesis and academic advisor. Maria will be the first in her family to graduate, and although her family is very supportive and encouraging, she has little access to individuals who have completed college and can offer her specific academic support and guidance. Maria and Professor Smith meet regularly to make sure Maria is fulfilling her academic requirements and meeting her thesis deadlines; however, Professor Smith notices Maria needs to develop her presentation and interview skills to be prepared for the graduate school admissions process. Professor Smith has reviewed her applications and provided feedback on personal statements. Behind the scenes, he has reached out to his colleagues at graduate programs, highlighting Maria's strengths as a candidate and her interpersonal skills. They meet at least weekly over lunch, in the lab or over coffee, to catch up on nonacademic happenings as Maria prepares to graduate and continue her academic and professional pursuits. Maria is an intelligent student with great potential, and the mentoring from Professor Smith is critical in her preparation for and success in gaining admission to competitive for selective graduate programs.

The short vignette highlights the important relationship between an undergraduate student and her mentor and provides an example of the features, form, structure, and types of support provided in the mentoring relationship. Confounding of relationships is just one of the many challenges mentoring researchers and practitioners are faced with when developing, implementing, and assessing mentoring efforts. The vignette highlights that characteristics may not only serve to identify a mentoring relationship but also may help in distinguishing mentoring from other developmental relationships prevalent in the academy (e.g., academic advising). Mentorship is about the choice to engage in such a relationship with the knowledge that the engagement will occur over a series of interactions and involve a variety of needed supports (Baker & Griffin, 2010).

Further, mentorship involves an emotional investment by both the mentor and protégé and a personal caring and commitment to the professional and personal development of the protégé. Both individuals have responsibility in the relationship and both are aware of and interested in pursuing a mentorship. In the vignette, Professor Smith offered Maria both career and psychosocial support, and both mentor and protégé were invested in Maria's positive outcomes. Professor Smith demonstrated emotional commitment beyond the communication of degree or other academic requirements, long-term care about Maria's professional and personal development, advocacy on her behalf, and a commitment to providing access to social capital through exposure to an academic network.

Access to social capital is particularly important when mentoring students from underrepresented groups, who are less likely to have networks of informed insiders investing in their success than those from majority populations. Based on the literature (see, e.g., Poteat, Shockley, & Allen, 2009), these characteristics are fundamental to effective mentoring relationships.

Who Can Be a Mentor?

Researchers have moved beyond the traditional view of mentoring, one in which a more senior organizational member provides mentorship to a new organizational entrant, to one that instead examines the variety of individuals who can provide mentoring supports, particularly in higher education settings. Based on years of research, it is clear that faculty members, staff members, graduate students, and peers are all important to college student success (Pascarella & Terenzini, 2005). In many cases, advisors, support staff members, administrative assistants, and graduate students share information with students or engage in task-specific exchanges, such as helping an undergraduate student understand a physics problem or ensuring appropriate forms have been submitted to meet departmental guidelines. The following section includes an overview of the four primary categories of individuals included in the mentoring model—discussed in further detail in the final chapter—who are likely to be instrumental to the experiences of undergraduate students.

Faculty Members

Faculty members are critical to the undergraduate student experience (Kim & Sax, 2009; Komarraju et al., 2010). Cole and Griffin (2013) concluded that "examining different forms or types of student–faculty interactions can promote a better understanding of the nature of student–faculty interactions and why they influence student outcomes" (p. 566). For the purposes of this monograph, two categories of faculty relationships are discussed: academic advisor and undergraduate research supervisor.

The academic advisor plays an important role in student success at the undergraduate level (Kuh, Kinzie, Schuh, & Whitt, 2011), particularly in predominantly teaching-focused institutions such as liberal arts colleges or community colleges. Academic advisors are responsible for helping students navigate institutional, departmental, and programmatic requirements. As Baker and Griffin (2010) wrote, "Advisors are expected to share their knowledge of major and degree requirements, help students schedule their courses, and generally facilitate progress to degree in a timely manner" (p. 3). Advisors also assist students in major and course selection and may write letters of recommendation for internships, scholarships, or off-campus study experiences. High-quality advising is associated with the sharing of complete and accurate information to advisees, clear guidance related to academic matters, and strong overall support with academic planning (Baker & Griffin, 2010).

Faculty can also engage students through the supervision of research. In her book, *The Good Supervisor*, Wisker (2012) characterized supervision of undergraduate research experiences as a highly prioritized teaching role and a critical context for student learning. She argued that research is a fundamental learning activity in which students develop problem-solving, decision-making, and analytical skills while engaging in knowledge creation and dissemination. Wisker asserted that undergraduate research supervision requires a great deal more structure and guidance compared to serving in such a capacity at the graduate student level. The supervisor helps the undergraduate researcher understand and engage in the research process as relevant to a given disciplinary domain (Baker, 2016) while also supporting other important skill development needed to successfully conceive of and engage in a research project such as time management, writing and presentation skills, and project management (Baker, 2016; Wisker, 2012).

Staff Members

Whereas faculty members are the individuals who deliver the educational experience in and out of the classroom, staff members also play a critical role in supporting undergraduate students' transition in college and advancement toward degree attainment. Academic advisors, counselors, student services personnel, and departmental administrative staff members often engage with students along their undergraduate journeys. Faculty members typically serve as the academic advisor in teaching-focused institutions; however, larger research-oriented institutions often employ staff members who meet with students to review course requirements, assist in course selection, and help monitor progress toward degree attainment.

Counseling and student services are important components of the academic experience, particularly during the first and final years of study (Pascarella & Terenzini, 2005; Rickinson, 1998). Professional counseling services and other areas of student support, such as a career development center, off-campus programming, and study abroad office, align with an integrated institutional approach to student support and are employed to varying degrees across institutions. Finally, departmental administrative staff can serve a significant function in the experiences of undergraduate students. They are responsible for communicating mass messages to enrolled students, sending reminders of departmental events, and helping to schedule meetings with faculty members. They are also the keepers of departmental forms, deadlines, and other pertinent information.

Graduate Students

Graduate students may be another category of individuals with whom undergraduate students interact during their collegiate experience, particularly in STEM fields in the form of lab technicians or research assistants. Although graduate students are not typically present in predominantly teaching-focused institutions such as liberal arts or community colleges, research universities often employ advanced doctoral students to serve as the instructor of record or as teaching assistants to support the efforts of faculty members. In these instances, undergraduate students may meet with teaching assistants for homework support or examination reviews during office hours. Further, graduate students may also play a central role as undergraduates engage in research, offering direction and instruction on lab techniques, data analysis, or the presentation of findings.

Peers

Relationships with peers may also serve as vital sources of social and academic support to students in college. Peer relationships and support have been suggested as particularly important for underrepresented and first-generation student populations and thus connect to the potential of mentoring programs to advance social justice. Peers can support one's decision to pursue a college degree; a lack of peer support and guidance can also negatively influence college adjustment (Dennis, Phinney, & Chuateco, 2005). More generally, researchers have noted that connecting with peers in authentic ways enriches the learning process, deepens a student's loyalty to the institution, and creates accountability for contributing in meaningful ways to the learning environment (Kuh et al., 2011).

Mentoring Literature Reviews

Robust research is needed to guide the development, implementation, and assessment of undergraduate mentoring efforts. There is a growing body of research investigating the forms, functions, and benefits of undergraduate mentoring relationships, and it can be difficult for practitioners and researchers to keep up with this rapidly expanding literature base. Literature reviews allow practitioners and researchers to synthesize and critically evaluate a large body of literature and thus to identify ideas for designing, implementing, and evaluating mentoring efforts that are grounded in empirical work. In the following paragraphs, we offer a summary of the most recent and relevant literature reviews focused on mentoring, which serve as a foundation and context for understanding the findings presented in this monograph.

Jacobi's (1991) foundational review highlighted the link between mentoring and undergraduate development and academic success. She identified mentoring as a critical component to undergraduate education. As previously mentioned, Jacobi's work brought attention to the absence of a common definition of mentoring. She concluded that mentoring exists in a variety of forms, characterized by factors such as duration and intensity. Jacobi also noted inconsistencies in findings across studies including the importance of pairing students with mentors who are the same gender or ethnicity. Importantly, Jacobi's review detailed limitations restricting the utility of findings. For instance, she noted a lack of empirically and theoretically based answers to questions about the nature of the relationship between mentoring and academic outcomes. The review also identified scholarship that incorrectly inferred a causal relationship between mentoring and student outcomes based on correlational research. Moreover, Jacobi noted that mentoring studies that focus on women and traditionally underserved groups were needed. Finally, she brought attention to the lack of research that assessed the prevalence of mentoring relationships within a postsecondary setting.

This review was followed 18 years later by Crisp and Cruz (2009), who provided a critical synthesis of empirical research conducted between 1990 and 2007. Overall, findings pointed to the potential of mentoring as a means to facilitate undergraduate students' adjustment and persistence in college. All but 2 of the 42 reviewed empirical studies identified a positive relationship between mentoring and one or more student outcomes such as GPA, persistence, and comfort with the university environment. Similar to Jacobi (1991), Crisp and Cruz's review identified numerous definitions of mentoring and found mentoring programs and efforts to function in various forms. The researchers also found that the majority of reviewed studies were program evaluations, with few enhancing understanding of the prevalence or outcomes from natural mentoring relationships. In contrast to the earlier review, Crisp and Cruz identified a growing number of programs tailored to specific populations and groups such as online students, athletes, and nursing students. Moreover, Crisp and Cruz found an expanded focus on programmatic efforts designed to serve groups who have been traditionally underserved in higher

TABLE 2
Persistent Limitations of the Mentoring Literature

Limitation Type	Description of Limitation
Conceptual	Inconsistencies in how mentoring is defined within an undergraduate context
	Lack of a clear description of what happens during mentoring relationships
	Need to understand why and how mentoring promotes development and success
	Lack of research focused on natural mentoring relationships
	Little work to understand experiences of mentors
	Institutional type rarely considered, little work outside 4-year institutions
Methodological	Limited attempts to control for confounding factors
	Very little work that controls for selection bias
	Overreliance on retrospective and correlational designs
	Need for longitudinal studies
	Small, nonrepresentative samples at a single campus
	Need for rigorous program evaluations
Theoretical	Absence of theory to guide mentoring research
	Lack of mentoring theory specific to a higher education context and/or undergraduate students
	Need for theory to guide the development, implementation and evaluation of mentoring programs

education, including racial/ethnic minorities and lesbian, gay, bisexual, trans*, and queer students.

Detailed in Table 2, Crisp and Cruz (2009) extended Jacobi's critique of the literature, identifying persistent conceptual, methodological, and theoretical weaknesses. The review found limited understanding regarding if, how, and why mentoring positively affects undergraduate students' development and academic success. There were few descriptions to foster understandings of what happens during mentoring relationships, as well as an absence of work that considered mentors' experiences. Crisp and Cruz further noted methodological limitations including limited attempts to control for confounding factors (e.g., other forms of support) and selection bias and the need for rigorous program evaluations (e.g., include comparison groups). The review also highlighted the absence of a conceptual or theoretical base to guide mentoring scholarship and programmatic efforts.

Monograph Purpose and Guiding Questions

The present monograph extends Crisp and Cruz's (2009) work by providing an updated, comprehensive review of research focused on mentoring undergraduate students. Crisp and Cruz identified 42 empirical studies that explicitly focused on mentoring students (both undergraduate and graduate) published between 1990 and 2007. Since that time, the body of mentoring literature has continued to grow, with 109 identified published empirical studies that focused on mentoring undergraduate students between 2008 and 2015. However, no attempt has been made to provide a systematic review of the mentoring literature since 2007, with the exception of Gershenfeld (2014), who reviewed a select number of studies focused specifically on formal mentoring programs published between 2008 and 2012.

It is unclear if or how the limitations in previous generations of mentoring research have been addressed by mentoring scholars or to what degree mentoring knowledge and theory has developed in recent years. As such, this monograph offers a review and synthesis of recent empirical studies focused on mentoring undergraduate students. The development and framing of the monograph was guided by the following questions:

1. In what ways did the empirical and theoretical understanding of mentoring as a means to develop and support undergraduate students advance between 2008 and 2015?
2. What characteristics serve to meaningfully distinguish mentoring relationships and programmatic efforts?
3. How can existing research and theory be integrated to explain the relationship between the various characteristics and outcomes of mentoring?
4. In what ways can recent empirical findings be applied to aid in the development, implementation, and evaluation of mentoring programs/efforts?

This review examines peer-reviewed qualitative and quantitative articles focused on mentoring undergraduate students published between 2008 and 2015. We searched the EBSCO, PsycEXTRA, Psychology and Behavioral Sciences Collection, SocINDEX with Full Text, and Education Full Text databases. In order to provide additional context for understanding mentoring relationships, the monograph also includes broader research on four prevalent types of undergraduate programs that commonly include a formal mentoring relationship. Additionally, we considered foundational and emerging theory and frameworks related to undergraduate students and/or mentoring (giving focus to articles published since 2008), which is used to both ground and contextualize empirical findings.

Monograph Overview

The next chapter of the monograph provides a synthesis and critique of the mentoring literature published between 2008 and 2015, organized by study focus and outcome. A key finding of the review is that mentoring relationships are increasingly studied and understood within the context of a formal mentoring program. As such, the third chapter identifies, describes, and compares the four most prevalent types of mentoring programs: (1) orientation and university retention programs, (2) mentoring for social justice and equity, (3) peer mentoring, and (4) undergraduate research and honors programs. The fourth chapter considers recent and foundational theoretical and conceptual models both in and outside of higher education, that serve to help understand undergraduate students' mentoring experiences and outcomes. The fifth chapter brings the central ideas presented in the monograph together by highlighting enduring limitations and areas for future research. The monograph concludes with a proposed integrated mentoring framework and evidence-based practices to support the efforts of mentoring scholars and practitioners moving forward.

Synthesis of Recent Empirical Findings

I N THIS CHAPTER, we provide an updated synthesis of empirical findings specific to mentoring undergraduate students, focusing on peer-
reviewed empirically based articles published since Crisp and Cruz's (2009)
review (i.e., between 2008 and 2015). We begin with general observations and
descriptions of the various components of the mentoring studies, including
research design and sample. Next, we provide a summary of findings organized by study focus and outcome. The chapter concludes with a summary
of how knowledge has been advanced in recent years.

Description of Reviewed Mentoring Scholarship

Consistent with prior reviews, we found that the majority of mentoring
research published between 2008 and 2015 focused specifically on formal
mentoring programs (see detailed descriptions in the third chapter). However,
roughly a third of the reviewed studies gave attention to studying *natural* mentoring relationships that undergraduate students may develop with faculty,
staff, and/or peers during the course of their college experiences. For instance,
research by Barnett (2011) brought attention to the value of validating mentoring relationships that develop informally between undergraduate students
and instructors. In contrast to prior reviews, we found an increasing focus
of mentoring efforts centering specialized or targeted student populations,
including African American students (e.g., Griffin, 2013), Latina/o students

(e.g., Tovar, 2014; Zell, 2009) and American Indian/Alaskan Native students (e.g., Guillory, 2009). At the same time, our review also identified mentoring studies that were more global, serving broader undergraduate populations such as first-year students. In terms of programmatic focus, we observed mentoring programs to be primarily directed toward STEM (e.g., Corso & Devine, 2013; Meyers, Sillim, Ohland, & Ohland, 2010), undergraduate research programs (e.g., Sams et al., 2015), and medical or nursing programs (e.g., Ketola, 2009; von der Borch et al., 2011). It is notable that STEM and undergraduate research programs are relatively well supported by federal agencies and that a common expectation associated with external grants is to conduct and disseminate program findings. As such, it is not surprising to find STEM and undergraduate research programs to be overrepresented in the mentoring literature.

Also consistent with previous reviews, the large majority of studies were focused on mentoring undergraduates who attend 4-year research institutions rather than community colleges or less selective (more accessible) 4-year universities. Exceptions include work by Corso and Devine (2013), Crisp (2009; 2010), and Zell (2009). Most studies appeared to be conducted at Predominantly White Institutions (PWIs), with relatively few focused on the experiences of students at Minority Serving Institutions. Additionally, the large majority of the reviewed studies were limited to mentoring experiences at a single institution. One of the potentially most generalizable studies was a study about leadership development by Campbell, Smith, Dugan, and Komives (2012) that included data collected from 101 institutions.

Although most reviewed mentoring studies did not use theory or a conceptual framework, a limited number were guided by theory, including Astin's college impact model (1993), social capital theory (e.g., Bourdieu, 1986), and mentoring models by Nora and Crisp (2007) and Kram (1988). (See a broader discussion of mentoring theory in the fifth chapter).

It is notable that most, but not all, studies did not distinguish between mentoring and other forms of supportive relationships such as advisors, institutional agents, advisors, developers, or coaches (e.g., Baker & Griffin, 2010; Bettinger & Baker, 2011; Museus & Neville, 2012; Tovar, 2014). Roughly half of the studies were directed toward undergraduate students' experiences with mentors who are faculty or staff. About a third of the reviewed studies were focused on peer mentoring relationships. Among these, Edgcomb et al. (2010) introduced the concept of near-peer mentors who are peer mentors close to the student in age and knowledge (e.g., students who are 1 year ahead in their studies). Additionally, many studies did not limit mentoring to a single individual but rather considered multiple sources of mentorship including faculty, staff, peers, supervisors, and family members (e.g., Crisp, 2010).

In terms of methodology, our review identified a healthy mix of qualitative and quantitative studies using diverse research designs and data collection techniques. Among the qualitative studies, case study methods and interviews were most commonly used to explore the benefits of mentoring, what mentoring looks like, and how it is experienced by students and mentors (e.g., Bell & Treleaven, 2010; Griffin, 2013). Qualitative methods were also used to explore students' and mentors' expectations of the mentoring relationship, as well as the perceptions, functions, and roles of mentoring. In quantitative studies, nonexperimental designs were most often used to test the relationship between mentoring and a variety of student outcomes. These studies largely relied on survey data and institutional student data, analyzed using various regression techniques. A small number of studies used quasi-experimental and experimental designs to compare participants with a matched group or randomly selected group of nonmentored students (e.g., Bettinger & Baker, 2011; Khazanov, 2011). The most common outcomes addressed by quantitative researchers include (a) college adjustment (Apprey et al., 2014; Meyers et al., 2010), (b) career and personal development (Haddock et al., 2013; Sams et al., 2015; Kinkel, 2011) and (c) measures of academic progress and success (Fox, Stevenson, Connelly, Duff, & Dunlop, 2010; Hu & Ma, 2010; Zell, 2009).

Mentoring Descriptions, Sensemaking, and Expectations

The reviewed studies collectively add to knowledge regarding what mentoring relationships look like, how students and mentors make sense of and meaning from their mentoring experiences, and what students and mentors expect from a mentoring relationship. Various research articles provided descriptions of different types of mentoring programs that can be used as models to develop mentoring programs at their respective institutions. For example, Bower and Bonnett (2009) offered a description of what mentoring looks like in the context of a physical education field experience. Apprey et al. (2014) provided a case study describing a cluster-mentoring model for Black undergraduate students that included four programmatic elements: (a) peer advising, (b) faculty mentoring and advising, (c) culturally sensitive initiatives, and (d) parental support.

Recent mentoring scholarship brings attention to the role of race and ethnic identity in how students and mentors make sense and meaning of mentoring relationships. For instance, Reddick and Pritchett (2015) sought to better understand cross-racial mentoring experiences between White faculty mentors and Black students. The findings of their qualitative study show faculty members perceive mentoring as a purposeful and iterative process of developing relationships with students. As a result of the mentoring experience, White mentors reported a heightened awareness of the unique challenges facing Black students attending a Predominantly White Institution. Similarly, Griffin (2013) sought to understand how Black professors made meaning of their interactions with Black students. Findings revealed that interactions between Black students and faculty mentors were different from interactions with students from other racial and ethnic groups in at least two ways. Black professors shared a unique commitment to Black students' success and experienced a sense of comfort and closeness with these students. Additionally, Ward et al. (2014) illuminated the meaning that American Indian students place on mentoring relationships with faculty members. The researchers found that non-Native instructors who engaged in authentic, caring interactions were able to successfully mentor American Indian students in a supportive tribal college context. Effective mentors developed trust and were able to support students' learning and personal goals. Importantly, findings also showed that successful mentoring strategies facilitated learning by doing and created opportunities for mentors to relate to Native students' worldview and context.

Recent studies have also highlighted the importance of understanding expectations and needs in the context of a mentoring relationship, or what Lunsford (2011) referred to as the *psychology of the mentoring relationship*. In sum, findings suggest that some students may be predisposed to benefit from a mentoring relationship (Henry, Bruland, & Sano-Franchini, 2011). For instance, results by Cox, Yang, and Dicke-Bohmann (2014) indicate that the effectiveness of mentoring may be dependent upon or moderated by the value students place on various mentoring functions. In this study, the cultural orientation of Hispanic students was a powerful predictor of how much students valued various mentoring functions, such as psychological support and role modeling. Additionally, the review of research revealed that not all students feel the need to be mentored (Lunsford, 2011). For instance, Larose et al. (2009) found mentoring to be more or less attractive for students based on several characteristics and background experiences including help-seeking attitudes, available support outside of the institution (e.g., parents), and academic disposition. Likewise, Lunsford (2011) found that students who were more certain in their career choice were more likely to report having a high-quality mentoring relationship.

Perceptions, Functions, and Roles of Mentoring

Since 2008, both qualitative and quantitative researchers have been engaged in studying how mentoring is perceived and the functions and roles that mentors play in supporting and guiding undergraduate students' academic pathways. Considering Nora and Crisp's mentoring framework (2007), recent studies show that mentoring may be perceived by undergraduate students to involve at least four types of interrelated forms of support: (a) psychological and emotional support, (b) degree and career support, (c) academic subject knowledge support, and (d) the existence of a role model. Crisp (2009) developed a survey to measure these forms of mentoring support titled the College Student Mentoring Scale (CSMS), which has been frequently used to measure how mentoring is perceived by various groups, including first-year students, community college students, and students attending Hispanic Serving Institutions (e.g., Crisp & Cruz, 2010; Henry et al., 2011).

This review also identified empirical research about the activities that mentors engage in with students and the various roles these activities play in promoting equitable outcomes. For instance, survey research by D'Abate (2009) suggested that faculty mentors perceived mentoring roles to include teaching, sharing information, advising, providing feedback, and setting academic goals. At the same time, faculty and peer mentors agreed that certain other roles such as modeling, affirming, befriending, and supporting may be best provided by peer mentors. Similarly, Bower and Bonnett's (2009) qualitative inquiry revealed five descriptors that characterize faculty mentors who teach in a physical education course: (a) a role model, (b) accepting and confirming, (c) a counselor, (d) a fun personality, and (e) a coach. Unfortunately, we found little research to understand the specific strategies or behaviors mentors implement to fulfill these roles or functions. One exception is a mixed-methods study by Lunsford (2011), which found that effective mentors provided career support to undergraduate students by taking them to conferences, involving them in research, and connecting them to other faculty.

Recent research revealed that the roles and functions of a mentoring relationship may vary across student populations and contexts, as undergraduate students are thought to construct meaning of their mentoring experiences in ways that are consistent with their lived experiences. For example, findings by Griffin and Reddick (2011) suggest that the nature of mentoring relationships and roles that mentors play may be different on the basis of gender. Specifically, the researchers found that Black women faculty were more likely to provide both instrumental and psychological support to students when compared to Black male faculty, who were more likely to engage with students in a more formal and less personal way. Using a feminist epistemological framework, Reilly and D'Amico (2011) sought to describe the role of mentoring for undergraduate women who had survived trauma. Four major themes emerged to describe the role of mentors that are both similar and different from other study populations: (a) fantasy mentors, (b) mentor as mirror, (c) mentor as nurturer and supporter, and (d) mentor as the embodiment of a profession.

Mentoring scholars have also recently begun to identify differences in students' and mentors' perceptions across racial and ethnic groups. A study of the Washington State Achievers (WSA) program by Hu and Ma (2010) found that Hispanic students were more likely to turn to their mentors for support and encouragement. Additionally, Hispanic students rated the importance of their overall experience with mentors higher than White students did. Similarly, research by Crisp (2009) revealed that various forms of mentoring support proposed by Nora and Crisp (2007) may be experienced differently between White, Hispanic, and African American students attending a community college. Further, research by Crisp and Cruz (2010) conducted at a 4-year Hispanic Serving Institution found that mentoring was experienced differently by White and Hispanic students, as evidenced by a significantly different factor structure.

The research we reviewed also identified differences in the expectations and perceptions of mentoring according to students' generational status. In particular, Mekolichick and Gibbs (2012) argued that first-generation students may approach mentoring from more of a utilitarian perspective (e.g., enhancing academic credentials) when compared to students whose family member(s) attended college. Continuing education students were more likely than first-generation students to expect to develop relationships with faculty members through a mentoring experience. Continuing education students were also more likely than first-generation students to view mentoring from a broader perspective, focusing on the personal and professional aspects of the relationship.

We also identified recent studies that examined mentoring roles and functions within specific programs and institutional contexts. Thiry, Laursen, and Hunter (2011) found that faculty mentors served an important function as role models of professional practice in the context of a STEM undergraduate research program. Interviews with racial minority students attending four PWIs revealed that students perceived effective institutional agents as engaging in the following activities: (a) sharing common ground with students, (b) offering holistic support, (c) humanizing the educational experience, and (d) offering proactive support (Museus & Neville, 2012). Similarly, Zell (2009) added to our understanding of what mentoring roles and functions look like in a community college context. In that study, faculty members played an important role as mentors and guides to community college students with regard to their career opportunities and professional options. Students relied on faculty mentors to access resources, navigate the campus including issues related to the transfer process, resolve academic difficulties, and discuss personal issues. Students also noted that discussions with faculty outside of class made them feel comfortable asking for help when needed and motivated them to pursue their goals.

It is important to note that the reviewed studies uncover that mentors' and students' perceptions of the mentoring experience may not always align. For instance, Holt and Berwise (2012) found that mentors reported providing a higher level of support than students perceived to have received from mentors, which was consistent across all dimensions of mentoring support. Similarly, Behar-Horenstein, Roberts, and Dix (2010) found that in contrast to the mentors' positive feedback, students indicated that mentors were not consistently and frequently available to students. At the same time, their findings also showed the groups had similar perceptions regarding the benefits of the mentoring experience, with both mentors and students observing mentoring to be beneficial to students in increasing their technical expertise and communication skills.

Mentoring Benefits

Despite evidence of some contradicting perceptions between mentors and protégés, findings from recent mentoring studies identify various benefits associated with mentoring—both for the mentor and the student. For example, research by Amaral and Vala (2009) suggested that peer mentors may directly benefit from mentoring. The researchers found that peer mentors earned higher grades and enrolled in more courses compared to students who had not participated as peer mentors. Similarly, Hryciw, Tangalakis, Supple, and Best (2013) found peer mentoring to be beneficial to both mentors and mentees. One particular benefit of mentoring to students was an increase in students' networks. Moreover, findings by Dolan and Johnson (2009) indicated that graduate students and postdoctoral associates also benefited from a mentoring relationship with undergraduate students. Graduate students and postdocs who mentored students experienced several gains including career preparation and improved teaching and communication skills.

Recent findings have also consistently shown benefits of mentoring for (a) undergraduates on the whole, (b) targeted groups of students, and (c) students enrolled in various types of programs and postsecondary institutional types. Kendricks and Arment (2011) found that mentoring activities created a nurturing environment for underrepresented minority students enrolled in a STEM-based scholars program. Students reported feeling safe, comfortable, and supported by their mentors. Moreover, in a study by Luna and Prieto (2009), Latina/o students reported several benefits from being mentored by graduate students and faculty including preparation for graduate school, expanded social networks, and sense of self-empowerment. Further, qualitative findings by Dahlvig (2010) indicated that relationships with mentors served as an encouragement to Black women at a Christian Predominantly White Institution.

At the same time, the benefits of mentoring may vary across programs and educational contexts. For instance, research by Shrestha, May, Edirisingha, Burke, and Linsey (2009) uncovered similarities and differences in the benefits for undergraduate students of an e-mentoring and face-to-face peer mentoring program. E-mentoring programs had benefits that face-to-face mentoring programs did not, such as flexibility and a lack of stigma. At the same time, however, e-mentoring programs had unique challenges, such as communication issues and the need for the mentor and mentee to have technological skills to maximize the benefits of the relationship. Findings by Slovacek et al. (2011) suggest that a particular benefit of mentoring to students enrolled in an undergraduate research programs (e.g., McNair Scholars, n.d.) may be the ability to obtain advice from the mentor about applying to graduate school. Additionally, specific to nursing programs, a literature review by Jokelainen, Turunen, Tossavainen, Jamookeeah, and Coco (2011) that examined 23 studies found that mentoring has at least two specific benefits for undergraduate nursing students. Mentoring facilitated students' learning by creating a supportive learning environment and strengthened students' professionalism by developing their identities and competence. Further, in one of the few studies to examine group mentoring, Kostovich and Thurn (2013) found that students who participated in a group mentoring experience uniquely benefitted by learning to work as a team. Additional work is needed to better understand the role of program design and educational context in shaping mentoring benefits and outcomes.

College Adjustment and Development

On the whole, the reviewed empirical evidence suggests that mentoring can help facilitate undergraduate students' transitions and adjustment during the first year of college. Fuentes, Alvarado, Berdan, and DeAngelo (2014) found that early interaction with faculty members helped socialize students to college and led to meaningful mentoring relationships with faculty in later years, affirming that early faculty interactions can develop into natural mentoring relationships. Similarly, pilot findings by Torres Campos and colleagues (2009) suggest that mentors can help Latina/o students identified as at risk adjust to college, as well as increase social support and awareness of resources. Results of a quasi-experimental research study examining the outcomes of peer mentoring programs in the United Kingdom by Collings, Swanson, and Watkins (2014) indicate that peer-mentored students showed higher levels of integration to university and were less likely than unmentored students to consider leaving the university. Findings suggest that mentoring may buffer the impact of students' transition issues. Further, although the study lacked a control group, an evaluation of a peer-mentoring program by O'Brien, Llamas, and Stevens (2012) suggests that mentored students may be less stressed about transitioning to the university and may be less concerned about not belonging due to those relationships.

Researchers have also recently examined the relationship between mentoring and outcomes related to students' motivations, efficacy, and career development. Holland, Major, and Orvis (2012) studied the role of peer mentoring and self-development activities in shaping students' commitment to science, technology, engineering, and mathematics (STEM) majors. Results indicate a positive relationship between peer mentoring and involvement in students' majors, satisfaction, and affective commitment. Recent research findings also suggest that mentoring may be positively related to self-efficacy. For instance, in an evaluation of an undergraduate STEM research program at four selective universities, students perceived that mentoring increased their confidence in professional their skills and abilities related to conducting research (Thiry,

Laursen, & Hunter, 2011). Additionally, although the research design did not include a control group, Kinkel (2011) found that students who participated in an e-mentoring program experienced gains specific to interest in career exploration, career awareness, and a willingness to relocate for career purposes.

Our review identified a limited amount of mentoring research focused on leadership and civic outcomes such as civic attitudes, social responsibility, and socially responsive leadership. Dugan and Komives' (2010) study focused on the mentoring experiences of college seniors. Grounded by the social change model of leadership development (Higher Education Research Institute, 1996), the researchers found that both faculty and peer mentoring relationships predicted measures of socially responsive leadership. Similarly, findings by Campbell et al. (2012) suggest that mentoring is positively related to students' leadership capacity. Results also suggest that students who have faculty mentors may benefit more from mentoring when compared to students who are mentored by student affairs mentors.

Academic Progress and Success

Consistent with the broader line of student-centered higher education research, the majority of the reviewed studies tested a relationship between mentoring and academic performance or success measures. Overall, findings suggest that mentoring is positively correlated with academic progress, persistence, and degree completion. Using a quasi-experimental design, Fox, Stevenson, Connelly, Duff, and Dunlop (2010) found that first-year students who participated in a university peer-mentoring program demonstrated better academic performance as compared to a similar group of nonparticipants. Kendricks, Nedunuri, and Arment (2013) uncovered that students enrolled in a STEM-focused scholars program indicated that mentoring was the largest contributing factor to their academic success. Our review also identified evidence of the effectiveness of mentoring in increasing students' academic performance, particularly for Latina/o students (e.g., Bordes-Edgar, Arredondo, Kurpius, & Rund, 2011). For instance, Tovar (2014) found that after controlling for pre-college factors, transition factors, and academic and social factors, time with faculty and counselors discussing career issues was positively related to Latina/o community college students' cumulative GPA.

We identified a good amount of research that focused on students' mentoring experiences and various academic success outcomes, such as persistence and degree completion. Schreiner, Noel, Anderson, and Cantwell (2011) studied the mentoring experiences of at-risk students across nine institutions. Students were asked to identify someone on campus who had been influential in their ability to remain enrolled in college. Interviews revealed mentoring roles that were perceived as most important in supporting students, including encouragement, motivation, taking time, expressing interest in students' successes, relating to students on their level, and balancing rigorous standards with support to succeed. Similarly, the majority of quantitative studies indicated that mentoring was related to students' intentions to persist, as well as their actual persistence behaviors (e.g., Barnett, 2011; Bordes-Edgar et al., 2011; Crisp, 2010, 2011; Hu & Ma, 2010; Khazanov, 2011). Most notably, results of a randomized control trial by Bettinger and Baker (2011) that involved mentoring nontraditional students across multiple universities revealed that students who were coached were more likely to persist to the second year of college. The treatment effect was particularly high for male students, suggesting that mentoring may be an effective means of reducing the gender gap in degree completion.

Although the majority of studies found mentoring to be positively related to academic outcomes, our review identified two studies that did not find significant mentoring effects. DeFreitas and Bravo (2012) did not find a relationship between informal faculty mentoring and academic achievement among underrepresented minority (URM) students attending a Hispanic Serving Institution (HSI). Similarly, a study of a National Institutes of Health (NIH) minority research training program by Schultz et al. (2011) did not find a significant relationship between having a "scientific mentor" and student intentions and persistence in science (p. 101).

Contributions of the Present Review

In comparison to previous literature reviews, we found that recent mentoring scholarship in some ways provides a more complex understanding of mentoring as a means to promote social justice and equity in higher education by more often focusing on student groups that have been historically under-studied and underserved in higher education. For example, roughly a fifth of the studies that we reviewed included mentoring programs that were specifi-cally focused on serving Latina/o, African American, Native American/Alaska Native, and/or low-income students. The qualitative and quantitative evidence from these studies help us to better understand how underserved populations experience mentoring, as well how mentoring may be positively related to various outcomes for students from these populations.

Empirical knowledge regarding the diversity and types of mentoring relationships has also advanced in recent years. Our review identified novel types of mentoring relationships that were not previously considered, including mentoring programs with an online or social media component (e.g., Chou, 2012) and group mentoring relationships with faculty and students (e.g., Kostovich & Thurn, 2013). We also found a number of studies that were focused on natural mentoring relationships (e.g., Barnett, 2011; Crisp, 2010), as the majority of work prior to 2008 had been largely limited to formal mentoring programs. We also noted a substantial increase in the number of empirical studies focused on peer mentoring programs, extending the understanding of mentoring beyond faculty–student relationships. The present review also identified more diversity in the outcomes that were considered by researchers in studying mentoring effects. Prior research and reviews focused on study-ing the impact of mentoring on undergraduate students' academic outcomes (grades and persistence specifically). Although a good number of studies ex-amined academic outcomes, we found less emphasis on these outcomes when compared to prior reviews, with more attention given to studying develop-mental outcomes such as career development and civic engagement. In this way, we found that recent work provides a more detailed understanding of the potential of mentoring as a developmental tool for undergraduate students.

In comparison to prior reviews, we also found that recent research gave more attention to theory, as well as what mentoring looks like and how it is perceived and experienced by undergraduate students. Researchers frequently used Nora and Crisp's (2007) conceptual model of mentoring to better understand the various types of support provided to students as part of a mentoring program or through natural mentoring relationships.

The present review also provides more knowledge than previously available describing mentoring programs and relationships, including the mentor matching process (Bell & Treleaven, 2010) and activities that mentors engage in with students (e.g., Lunsford, 2011). Moreover, our review advances understanding of how different groups of students and mentors may perceive mentoring differently (e.g., Crisp, 2009; Crisp & Cruz, 2010; Hu & Ma, 2011; Mekolichick & Gibbs, 2012).

Summary and Conclusions

The reviewed empirical studies published between 2008 and 2015 collectively add to the preexisting body of evidence that mentoring can be an effective means of addressing the Completion Agenda and other national efforts by contributing to undergraduate students' success. In particular, findings reveal that mentoring can effectively support students' development, adjustment to college, motivations, efficacy, career development, leadership skills, grades, persistence, and degree completion. Benefits appear to hold for undergraduate students on the whole as well as for students who have been traditionally underserved in higher education and for students who remain underrepresented in particular academic fields (e.g., STEM). Beyond identifying the potential beneficial outcomes of mentoring, this synthesis highlights rich descriptions regarding the characteristics of mentoring (e.g., functions, sources, and forms of support), which have practical implications. Additionally, study findings add details about what mentoring looks like in particular programs and institution types was well as how different types of students and mentors make sense and meaning from their relationships, which have direct application for mentoring practice (as discussed in the fifth chapter).

Contextualizing Mentoring Relationships

THIS CHAPTER HIGHLIGHTS the influences of context and purpose on mentoring programs and relationships. The context and organizational environment exert considerable influence on undergraduate mentoring relationships by driving the goals, expected outcomes, and structure of mentoring experiences (Lunsford, 2016). The literature reviewed in the previous chapter identified an increase in the number of studies that have examined formal mentoring programs. This chapter revisits that literature, describing the most common types of programmatic initiatives that have been shown to promote student development and academic success. In particular, the reviewed literature points to four types of undergraduate mentoring programs: (a) orientation and first-year experience programs; (b) mentoring for social justice and equity; (c) peer mentoring programs; (d) and undergraduate research and honors programs that include a mentoring component. We provide insights into the distinguishing characteristics of each type of program in terms of focus and purpose, program characteristics, program forms and structures, and intended goals and/or outcomes.

Orientation and Retention Programs

In the following section, we provide an overview of orientation, first-year experience, and retention programs for undergraduate

students and the role of mentoring in such experiences. Institutional
and individual outcomes are noted.

Program Focus and Purpose

Orientation programs, first-year experience programs, and/or retention programs often include a formal mentoring component (Bean & Eaton, 2001; Pascarella & Terenzini, 2005). The purpose of such programs is to help students manage the transition from high school to college, during which homesickness, time management, social pressures, and differing learning styles may negatively influence students' experiences (Michael, Dickson, Ryan, & Koefer, 2010; Salinitri, 2005). Orientation, first-year experience, and retention programs offer techniques to help students overcome these transition challenges. The ultimate aims of these programs are to increase academic and social integration and to provide students with the tools to be self-sufficient as they progress toward graduation. Although such programming is available to all students, colleges and universities also offer special programming aimed to support targeted populations of students, such as academically low-performing students (Salinitri, 2005), first-generation students (Reid & Moore, 2008), and those from underrepresented minority populations (Hurtado et al., 2008); the latter category is discussed later in the chapter.

Program Characteristics

Institutional policies and practices clearly have an impact on student retention; as one type of institutional effort, orientation and retention programs are expected to change student behavior by increasing retention (Bean & Eaton, 2001). Bean and Eaton offered an interactionist perspective of retention, whereby students' psychological attributes, as shaped by their experiences and abilities, interact with the institution, its representatives, and the academic and social realms. These interactions trigger students' self-assessments in terms of academic and social integration (or lack thereof), which can encourage them to use the adaptive strategies learned through orientation and retention programs. Such strategies include study skills, effective communication approaches, time management, organizational tools, and managing emotions. Specific programs such as the New Student Services Orientation at the

University of California at Berkeley train students to work more effectively with peers and to develop effective study habits and other coping strategies (http://nss.berkeley.edu/). These programs welcome students to campus, expose them to more advanced students as mentors and role models, and help socialize them to campus life.

Program Form and Structure

Students experience orientation, first-year experience, and retention programs in a variety of forms. A notable form in the literature is living–learning communities, in which students take the same courses and engage in activities within a residential setting, such as an on-campus house or a particular section of a residence hall (Inkelas, Daver, Vogt, & Leonard, 2007). Often, activities are centered on a particular topic or theme. Students also use these settings to talk about transition concerns and ways to manage academics as well as social aspects of the undergraduate student experience. These living–learning programs are often supported by institutional staff and faculty members who serve as mentors (Cambridge-Williams, Winsler, Kitsantas, & Bernard, 2013). In addition, students are expected to benefit from peer mentoring in these communities, as discussed later in this chapter.

Expected Outcomes

According to Inkelas and Soldner (2011), as well as Lotkowski, Robbins, and Noeth (2004), the expected outcomes of orientation, first-year experience, and retention programs may be to develop academic skills (i.e., writing, study habits, and quantitative reasoning), self-confidence, institutional commitment, and social support. Students who engage in living–learning programs have been shown to display higher levels of engagement in college activities and stronger academic outcomes than their non-participating peers (Inkelas et al., 2007). The peer-to-peer connection is an important one that facilitates the first-year transition through the creation of social and academic supports (Kift, 2009). As the name implies, persistence and timely degree completion are also goals of retention programs.

Mentoring for Social Justice and Equity

Given the increase in research and practice of mentoring to support social justice and equity, the following section features programs aimed to support underrepresented groups' academic and social development.

Program Focus and Purpose

Our review identified over 20 articles (roughly one fifth of the reviewed studies published since 2008) that described programs explicitly targeted toward mentoring programs for African American, Latina/o, and/or American Indian or Alaska Native populations. The purposes of mentoring programs for students from historically underrepresented groups are to recruit, support, and retain students to degree completion, as well as to encourage and support transitions into professional roles or graduate studies. At their core, these mentoring programs reflect a social justice orientation where a key aim is to reduce inequities in developmental and academic outcomes. The aims of these programs are to increase a sense of empowerment, well-being, and self-determination among underrepresented students (Evans & Prilleltensky, 2007). For example, the Posse Program (Posse Foundation, n.d.) grants scholarships to public high school students through its partnerships with colleges and universities and places recipients in groups of 10 (or posses) as a strategy for cultivating peer support throughout their undergraduate experiences. At the next stage in the educational pipeline, the Ronald E. McNair Scholars Program provides 151 colleges and universities with federal funding to prepare first-generation students and those from underrepresented racial/ethnic groups for doctoral studies through firsthand experiences with research and scholarship under the guidance of a faculty member (McNair Scholars, n.d.). Another example is the Meyerhoff Scholarship Program at the University of Maryland, Baltimore County, founded in 1988. Research about this program has demonstrated that intent to earn a STEM Ph.D. was substantially increased among undergraduate students from underrepresented minority groups who had participated in supervised research activity (Carter, Mandell, & Maton, 2009).

Program Characteristics

Mentoring programs for social justice and equity can be characterized by activities that combine academic, emotional, and sociocultural support from peers as well as graduate students, faculty, and staff. These programs may address the needs of students who are the first in their family to attend college and who did not have access to important cultural capital or knowledge of what promotes success in the campus environment. Rios-Ellis et al. (2015) described an example of such a mentoring program for Latino students who attend California State University, Long Beach, which was designated as a Hispanic Serving Institution in 2005. Drawing from cultural capital and critical race theories and the "*promotores* (lay peer educators) model" found in some Latin American and Caribbean countries, the *Promotores de Educación* program prepared higher performing Latino students to serve as peer mentors. The *promotores* provided their peers with academic and personal support and also helped them to engage with university services (Rios-Ellis et al., 2015, p. 42).

Program Form and Structure

Mentoring programs for students from underrepresented groups address the combination of needs these students may have beyond the general challenges associated with transitioning to college, as an effort to advance social justice and equity. These programs provide experiences to support academic success, and to enhance social and emotional support and community-building. A combination of academic and cocurricular activities supports students academically and socially. Programs may provide students with partners from near peers to senior faculty members to support their knowledge of the opportunities available through degree completion and their sense of themselves as potential entrants into the professions and disciplines (Wilson et al., 2012).

Expected Outcomes

Mentoring programs for social justice and equity are explicitly or implicitly designed to promote social justice and equity by increasing persistence and degree completion rates for African American, Latina/o, and/or American Indian and Alaska Native populations. Recent findings suggest that effective mentoring programs and those targeted for students from underrepresented minority groups can be effective in generating positive outcomes for students, such as increased engagement, feelings of integration in to the college environment (Collings, Swanson, & Watkins, 2014), and academic performance (Shojai, Davis, & Root, 2014). Programs have also been shown to cultivate students' knowledge of—and sense of fit within—graduate training and the professions (Wilson et al., 2012).

Peer Mentoring

An important component across the programs featured in this chapter and through this monograph are the presence of peers as important to the overall student experience and as mentors themselves. In the following section, we discuss peer mentoring programs while acknowledging the presence and importance of peer mentors across a variety of formal and informal mentoring programs.

Program Focus and Purpose

Peer mentoring programs match a more experienced student with a less experienced student. Peers may be matched based on individual characteristics such as race or socioeconomic class; however, there are also peer mentoring programs focused on supporting students as they achieve academic or professional goals without consideration of demographic characteristics. As mentioned in the previous chapter, roughly a third of the reviewed studies included a formal peer mentoring component. Peer mentoring programs seek to provide academic, career, and/or psychosocial development to undergraduate students through the provision of guidance from a more experienced student. Such programs facilitate mentoring relationships with peers who are only slightly more experienced and have been established as an effective practice (Terrion & Leonard, 2007). For example, peer mentoring is advocated by the National Collegiate Honors Council as a mechanism to orient new students to college life, outside of the faculty purview (Peer Mentoring, n.d.).

Program Characteristics

Peer mentoring programs focused on supporting students' academic development have been developed and assessed across a range of institutional and individual characteristics. Individually, this may include students' race and ethnicity, major, or career goals. Institutionally, areas of focus include profession or discipline (e.g., Holland et al., 2012). Within the academic disciplines, there is a prevalence of peer mentoring programs in STEM fields (e.g., Budny, Paul, & Newborg, 2010). Programmatic areas of focus extend beyond the discipline or profession to other aspects of undergraduate education, such as undergraduate research, which is described later in this chapter.

Program Form and Structure

A mere willingness to provide support does not seem to be sufficient in and of itself for a successful relationship. Similarity in program of study and mentors' evidence of maturity, life experience, and initial college success are important in mentor selection. Further, Terrion and Leonard (2007) found that peer mentors are effective when protégés perceive that support from their mentors is readily available to them, regardless of the time spent on mentoring. Additional characteristics of effective peer mentors include having their own high goals, effective communication skills, trustworthiness, empathy, flexibility, and a general enthusiasm for the mentoring program and their roles in it (Terrion & Leonard, 2007).

Expected Outcomes

Academic and career-related functions are more limited in peer relationships than traditional mentor–protégé relationships; however, peer mentors offer strong support and fulfill psychosocial functions such as confirmation, emotional support, feedback, and friendship (Terrion & Leonard, 2007). Present findings show that mentoring programs can be valuable for both the mentoring students and those they mentor. Students who are mentored by peers may experience benefits including increased motivation for academic success, academic skills, and familiarity with the college environment. Those who serve as peer mentors have also been found to benefit through the development of professional and leadership skills, as well as increased confidence and the ability to see themselves as leaders and professionals as they prepare for the next stage of their own journeys (Zevallos & Washburn, 2014).

Undergraduate Research and Honors Programs

Given an increase in UR experiences across all institution types, we discuss the role of mentoring in supporting and facilitating undergraduate students' experiences as they engage in undergraduate research, scholarship, and creative inquiry.

Program Focus and Purpose

Formal mentoring of undergraduate research (commonly referred to as UR) experiences can be separated into two types of programs with different yet overlapping aims. First, there are nationally funded programs, such as the National Science Foundation Research Experiences for Undergraduates, that allocate funds for UR at the institutional level (https://www.nsf.gov/crssprgm/reu/). The purpose of these programs is to reduce racial/ethnic disparities in graduate education (Schultz et al., 2011) and to retain students in fields seen as needing more graduates, including STEM (Kendricks et al., 2013). Although undergraduate research experiences and corresponding mentorship have been situated predominantly in STEM fields, the importance of and interest in undergraduate research including best practices for mentors in other disciplines is increasing. The journal *Perspectives on Undergraduate Research and Mentoring* (PURM) recently published a special issue on mentoring undergraduate research in the professional disciplines (Issue 5.1), examining the role of mentors and undergraduate research as an innovative pedagogical tool. Additionally, organizations such as the Council on Undergraduate Research host annual conferences with participants and presenters from a range of disciplines.

The second type of undergraduate research program includes institutionally sponsored undergraduate research programs designed to meet the institution's mission. For instance, the Showcase for Undergraduate Research

TABLE 3

Categorization of Undergraduate Research Experiences by Dimensions of Who, How, and What

Category	Dimension
Who	All vs. honors students
	Individual vs. collaborative
How	Process vs. outcome
	Student initiated vs. faculty initiated
What	Curriculum vs. cocurricular fellowships
	Original to student vs. discipline
	Interdisciplinary vs. discipline based
	Campus community vs. professional audience

and Creative Activities (SURCA) program at Washington State University provides experiences with a mentor as well as a space for students across majors to present their research. Similarly, mentoring undergraduate students is often a core value of liberal arts colleges, which have been at the forefront of integrating UR into their programming, despite their historical emphasis on the liberal arts over professional preparation. Yet another example is the mentoring that takes place in institutionally supported honors or scholars programs (Lunsford, 2011), which are in many cases an enrollment management tool established to recruit academically talented students. Mentoring may also take place as part of honors theses or other projects in the college or department (Anderson, Lyons, & Weiner, 2014). It is also notable that a number of UR programs offer funding specifically for minority serving institutions as a means of promoting social justice and equity (e.g., Davis, 2010; Dodson, Montgomery, & Brown, 2009).

Program Characteristics

In the present review, Beckman and Hensel (2009) characterized undergraduate research mentoring by eight dimensions. We group these dimensions into three overarching categories that address the target populations (who), processes (how), and goals (what) of the mentoring experience (see Table 3). Under the "who" category, there are two dimensions. Some UR experiences are open to any interested students whereas other programs are limited to honors students who engage in UR through a thesis or capstone requirement. Programs are also set up to focus on individual research (e.g., through an independent study) in contrast to collaborative research that involves a team of students through a class or group lab project.

Under the "how" category, UR programs reflect differences in the initiation and process of the experience. A process-focused experience directs students' attention to the steps of scholarly inquiry in a discipline, such as how to conduct a literature review, design a research question, collect relevant evidence, and analyze and interpret results. Students are typically assessed by how well they understand and master these steps. In contrast, a focus on outcomes means that students must produce a product, such as a presentation of their work at a poster session or submission of a manuscript to a journal. The crafting or initiation of the experience is a second "how" dimension. In some experiences, faculty might recruit students to participate in an ongoing research project the faculty member has designed, whereas other UR experiences are initiated by students based on their interests. Undergraduate research is built into the curriculum in some majors or at some institutions. One example is the discipline of psychology, in which undergraduates must take required methods and statistics courses and engage in research as part of the courses. Another example of curricular experiences would be receiving credit for independent studies. In contrast, a summer research program without academic credit would be an example of a cocurricular fellowship.

Finally, the "what" category varies in originality, discipline, and audience. Research expectations for originality may be unique to the discipline or a discovery experience for the student through a replication project not unique to the discipline. Some UR experiences are grounded in a discipline, such as chemistry or history, whereas other experiences require students to integrate information from more than one discipline. Finally, students' efforts and achievements are evaluated differently if the audience is their classroom or campus, such as a presentation in an academic sphere, versus a presentation to a professional audience, such as a case competition demonstrating how an engineering or business problem might be solved.

Program Form and Structure

UR mentoring involves a relationship between a student and a research mentor. Faculty members (Craney et al., 2011; Lunsford, 2011), graduate students (Dolan & Johnson, 2009), or advanced undergraduate students (Ochoa, Lunsford, Minera, & Fosmire, 2015) have been found to effectively serve as research mentors. These mentoring experiences provide opportunities for students to work on research teams to learn how scholarly inquiry takes place in their disciplines. Students may be involved in basic tasks, such as coding data or running experiments for others, or more complex tasks, such as analyzing data or conducting an independent inquiry related to the research enterprise (Baker, Pifer, Lunsford, Greer, & Ihas, 2015).

Expected Outcomes

Schultz et al. (2001) found that participation in undergraduate research experiences increased students' intent to pursue science as compared to a matched control group. Further, participation in UR was shown to explain students' interest in persisting in a science major. Engagement in UR has also been shown to be positively associated with higher grade point averages (Fechheimer, Webber, & Kleiber, 2011) and intentions to persist in fields such as science (Schultz et al., 2011) and counseling psychology (Van Vliet, Klingle, & Hiseler, 2013). Improved selection of research problems (Craney et al., 2011) is another identified benefit to students who engage in undergraduate research. In addition, UR experiences have been associated with greater self-efficacy and scientific literacy (Hunter, Laursen, & Seymour, 2007; Russell, Hancock, & McCullough, 2007), particularly summer research experiences for students in STEM fields (Chemers, Zurbriggen, Syed, Goza, & Bearman, 2011; Lopatto, 2007).

As noted previously, some programs were shown to only focus on honors students. The outcomes for such programs were identifying with an intellectual community, choice of vocation, and increased self-efficacy. Lunsford (2011) found student identity commitment was positively associated with high-quality mentoring experiences. For example, studies have found increases in professional and personal growth for honors students who participate in UR (Hébert & McBee, 2007; Stanford & Shattell, 2010). It is notable that most studies were shown to focus on outcomes for the student mentee.

TABLE 4
Contexts, Purposes, Characteristics, Form and Structure, and Outcomes of Mentoring Programs

Context	Purpose	Characteristics	Form and Structure	Expected Outcomes
Orientation and retention	Transition to college	Academic and social skills	Cocurricular, living–learning communities	Retention and persistence, engagement
Underrepresented minority	Degree completion, persistence to graduate studies or profession	Academic, emotional, and sociocultural support	Academic and cocurricular	Retention and persistence. engagement, academic performance
Peer mentoring	Academic, career, and/or psychosocial development	Socialization to college, discipline, or program	Academic and cocurricular	Retention, engagement, academic performance
Research and honors	Prepare a diverse workforce, institutional recruitment	Disciplinary knowledge, research process	Curricular: thesis, independent study, class; Cocurricular: reading or social groups	Retention, GPA, research self-efficacy, belonging

However, studies have also identified benefits to mentors (Baker et al., 2015), such as improved mentoring skills and greater enjoyment of their own relationship with their mentor (Dolan & Johnson, 2009; Hurtado et al., 2008).

Should the Table 4 reference go in the summary or do we need a short section noting Table 4 summarizes the program categories featured in this chapter? I include the below in case you prefer the latter

This chapter features the four most common types of mentoring program prevalent in undergraduate student experiences. Table 4 summarizes the context, purpose, characteristics, form and structure, and outcome of the programs discussed in this chapter.

Summary and Conclusions

Formal mentoring programs for undergraduates are ubiquitous on college campuses. Mentoring programs are supported by national and institutional partners who have expected goals to recruit, retain, and graduate students who participate in them. This chapter serves to contextualize findings presented in the previous chapter by highlighting similarities and differences in the purposes, structures, and expected outcomes of the four most prevalent types of mentoring programs: (a) orientation/retention, (b) social justice, (c) peer mentoring, and (d) research/honors. Similar to the definitions of mentoring discussed in the first chapter, we find that distinguishing mentoring programs into groups provides a somewhat imprecise typology, with a sizable amount of overlap across and between program types. For example, the McNair Scholars program provides mentoring to underrepresented minority students through undergraduate research experiences.

However, the organization of the contexts and purposes between programs may provide scholars and practitioners tools to think about how to best develop programming that will support their target populations and outcomes, as well as how to assess the effectiveness of mentoring programs given their stated purposes. For instance, it may benefit program managers who run orientation or first-year mentoring programs to evaluate carefully if they are achieving the desired program goals. Relatedly, by thinking of mentoring programs for underrepresented populations as social justice programs, the goals might then focus on reduction of inequitable outcomes rather than considering the number of minority student participants. Desired outcomes are related to a successful transition to college and a sense of belonging and confidence that will lead to degree completion and persistence to graduate school or professions. Researchers might also benefit from more clearly linking the contexts for mentoring programs to expected student outcomes to determine if the programs and concomitant resources are being used as well as they could be. Student success and sense of belonging can be supported through mentoring programs that focus on engagement in the academic community, academic and social skill enhancement, strategies to manage institutional expectations, and emotional intelligence and coping skills.

Established and Emerging Mentoring Frameworks

A COMMON CRITIQUE of mentoring scholarship inside and outside of higher education is that it is rarely grounded in or used to generate theory (Jacobi, 1991; Johnson, Rose, & Schlosser, 2007). Retention and involvement frameworks (e.g., Astin, 1984, 1993; Tinto, 1993) highlight the importance of student–faculty interaction generally, and mentorship specifically, in fostering student success. However, these frameworks do not provide insight into how mentoring is distinguished from other relationships, what happens within the context of mentoring relationships, or why and how mentoring relationships bring about specific academic, social, and career development outcomes. In other words, although we have the sense that mentorship "works" in terms of promoting student outcomes, there is little understanding of the parameters that define these relationships, the mechanisms undergirding mentoring, or what it is about mentorship that brings about more positive social, educational, and career outcomes. Without this knowledge, it is difficult to conduct research that will ultimately inform mentoring programs and practices that reliably and consistently promote positive undergraduate student outcomes.

In this chapter, we consider theoretical and conceptual models that focus explicitly on mentoring and thus help scholars and practitioners to better understand the structure, nature, and outcomes of these relationships. We incorporate models included in current undergraduate mentoring research in higher education with frameworks from business and psychology to offer a more comprehensive understanding of the unique contributions mentoring theory can make to higher education research, deepening our understanding of relationship dynamics and outcomes to inform mentoring practices.

Overview of Mentoring Theories and Frameworks

Despite a lack of a coherent body of mentoring theory, individual researchers have been creative in integrating or drawing upon interesting and innovative frameworks. For example, scholars have developed conceptual models to guide their work, translating established theory and scholarship about retention, social engagement, leadership, motivation, and belonging to the study of mentorship (e.g., Apprey et al., 2014; Dugan & Komives, 2010; Gross, Iverson, Willett, & Manduca, 2015; Zell, 2009). In some cases, researchers have leveraged organizational change literature or scholarship about community development to address the formation of and benefits associated with mentoring relationships (e.g., Chou, 2012; Noufou, Rezania, & Hossain, 2014). Although these studies and integrative models have much to offer, the models presented are seldom integrated more widely into mentoring scholarship and are largely unique to the specific studies for which they were developed. This review instead focuses on frameworks more widely used in literature on undergraduate education, mentoring, and student experiences. We organize frameworks into three categories. First, we review frameworks that offer ways to define and categorize mentoring relationships. This is followed by an overview of frameworks that aim to explain what motivates and happens within mentoring relationships. Finally, we present frameworks that offer insight into the relationship between mentoring and student outcomes.

Typology-Related Frameworks

In addition to work that aims to synthesize and identify a consistent definition of "mentor" or "mentorship," some scholars have proposed frameworks that provide insight into the functions or typologies of developmental relationships. There is an emerging collection of frameworks that may help scholars and practitioners recognize what mentoring is and the resources mentoring relationships potentially provide.

Multiple frameworks organize the factors, dimensions, or components that, when present, define a mentoring relationship. For example, Tentoni (1995) adapted Anderson and Shannon's (1988) work to the mentorship of counseling students and identified mentoring as teaching, sponsoring, encouraging, counseling, and befriending. Jacobi's (1991) review of the literature identified five characteristics that defined mentoring relationships in educational settings, which are offered as a foundation for the development of mentoring theory and research. First, mentoring is defined as a helping relationship focused on helping a protégé meet long-term goals. The nature of mentoring relationships differs but includes emotional support, direct assistance and career development, and role modeling to varying degrees. Third, mentoring relationships are reciprocal. These relationships are personal, requiring direct interaction. Finally, mentors are individuals with more experience, knowledge, and influence than their protégés.

Kram's (1988) work is foundational in the development of frameworks that aim to capture what mentoring is and the specific dimensions of these relationships. Although grounded in a business perspective and context, Kram's work has been frequently adapted and applied to higher education. Kram identified the functions of developmental relationships, or aspects of the relationship that promote growth and development. Although there are many potential functions, Kram consolidated them into two categories: career and psychosocial. Career functions are related to professional socialization and development and include exposing protégés to important networks, facilitating skill development, and offering protection from unnecessary risks. The psychosocial functions reflect relationship quality and are connected to building protégé identity and sense of self-worth. Counseling, friendship, acceptance, and positive feedback within mentoring relationships can translate to a mentee's sense of worth and efficacy. Although both are important to navigating challenges and career progression, relationships vary in their incorporation of these functions. Kram's review of the literature suggested that relationships that incorporate both career and psychosocial functions lead to stronger connections and success that goes beyond the immediate workplace (or in the case of higher education, the college campus).

Recent work incorporated and expanded on Kram's (1988) career and psychosocial functions of mentoring relationships. Crisp and colleagues (Crisp, 2009; Crisp & Cruz, 2009; Nora & Crisp, 2007) offered a framework that focuses on the forms of assistance to which students gain access through mentoring relationships. Although there is some conceptual overlap with Kram's (1988) work, this framework is specific to higher education and the needs and goals of students. Based on a synthesis of existing research and their own empirical work, Crisp and colleagues propose four constructs of undergraduate mentoring relationships: psychosocial and emotional support, degree and career support, academic subject knowledge support, and the existence of a role model. Psychosocial and emotional support shares much in common with Kram's psychosocial mentoring function and addresses encouragement, understanding, and active empathetic listening within the relationship. Degree and career support focuses on the assessment of a student's strengths and weaknesses as well as the development of longer term goals and strategies to reach them. Academic subject knowledge support addresses skill development in a specific area of study. The final component incorporates access to a role model as well as the ability to learn from a mentor's successes and failures. Ishiyama's (2007) Mentor Role index incorporates three similar measures, assessing how much students' value career support, research/academic support, and personal consideration in their mentoring relationships.

Mertz (2004) offered a conceptual model that distinguishes between different types of relationships in higher education, organizing relationships into a pyramid based on intent, with psychosocial development at the bottom, professional development in the middle, and career advancement at the top. Six specific roles are identified at each level, differentiated by required involvement. By incorporating an involvement dimension, this framework emphasizes that mentors and protégés can engage in a limited number of high-involvement relationships. Psychosocial development is the focus of relationships at Levels 1 and 2, requiring the lowest levels of involvement. Relationships at Levels 3 and 4 focus on professional development, and Levels 5 and 6 address career advancement. The mentor resides at Level 6, the top of the hierarchy, requiring the most significant level of involvement, clear future orientation, and fundamental focus on making professional strides in and outside of an organization. The role of mentor is differentiated from those of counselor, advisor, or guide, which reside at Level 3; Level 3 relationships have a different intent (professional development) and level of investment.

Higgins and Kram (2001) offer a typology developed out of research in business that shifts focus from individual mentoring dyads to the multiple relationships protégés form to gain access to support, which they label developmental networks. Higgins and Kram suggested that there is diversity within the kinds of mentoring relationships people form and that no one person can provide all of the resources necessary to facilitate career advancement and success. Thus, individuals form networks of people who are focused on providing them with information and support. Developmental networks are differentiated based on their diversity, or the extent to which supporters are from different social spheres, and strength of relationships. More diverse networks provide individuals with a less redundant and broader range of information. Stronger ties often mean more intimacy and stronger investment in the protégé's career development. Although acknowledging that these criteria are more often on continua rather than discrete categories, Higgins and Kram identified four kinds of developmental networks based on degrees of diversity and strength: entrepreneurial, traditional, receptive, and opportunistic. Traditional networks are not very diverse, but members have strong relationships. Alternatively, high levels of diversity and strong ties between members mark entrepreneurial networks. Opportunistic networks also are very diverse but tend to have weak ties and members may be less invested in cultivating relationships. Receptive networks are less diverse and have weak ties. These networks may provide weak support and often contain redundant information.

Process-Based Frameworks

Mentoring research is also limited by a lack of theoretical work establishing what happens within relationships, factors that motivate engagement between mentors and mentees, or how identity governs the nature of interaction. There are fewer frameworks offering insight in this area; however, some work has been done to explain what happens within developmental relationships.

Some theories have aimed to capture the phases or stages through which relationships progress (Hunt & Michael, 1983; Kram, 1988; Zachary, 2002). Stage models allow scholars and practitioners to acknowledge the changing nature of mentoring relationships, creating the opportunity to understand the need for and ultimately provide specific forms of interaction and resources based on where mentors and mentees are in their relationship. Kram (1988) suggests mentoring relationships progress through four phases: initiation, cultivation, separation, and redefinition. Shifts in phase are marked by the needs, concerns, and development of the mentor or protégé, as well as organizational forces or pressures. Initiation represents the beginning of a relationship, marked largely by positive emotions, high expectations for the quality of the relationship, and increasing closeness. The cultivation phase is also generally positive, and it is during this phase that the career and psychosocial functions of the relationship are highly present. The mentee develops competence and confidence, and the relationship becomes increasingly close and reciprocal. Separation is initiated as the protégé's and mentor's goals and needs shift. The relationship in its current form ends, which is often marked by some degree of anxiety and sadness. In the final phase, redefinition, the relationship reemerges, sometimes years later, in a new form, when the relationship becomes more of a friendship.

Whereas Kram's (1988) phase model was developed based on a study of business professionals, Zachary (2002) offered a four-phase model specific to education. Zachary's model shares characteristics with Kram's, such as acknowledgment of a beginning and closure to a relationship, but the phases are more focused on the behaviors that will facilitate success and movement to the next phase. The first phase, preparing, requires mentors and protégés to assess their skills and readiness, as well as what motivates them to form the relationship, through careful reflection and intentional conversations. Negotiating is reliant upon open communication and conversation as mentors and protégés agree on learning goals and define what will happen within the context of the relationship. Enabling is the longest phase and provides the greatest opportunity for learning and vulnerability to challenges. Mentors and protégés must work together to define the unique nature of their own relationship and work toward goals. Finally, in closure, the relationship comes to an end, which may create anxiety but also creates opportunities for mentors and protégés to evaluate their learning and celebrate their achievements.

Scholars have also presented frameworks that provide insights into the qualities or characteristics necessary to have a successful mentoring relationship that supports a protégé's career development. Although focusing on mentoring in graduate education, Johnson's (2003) triangular model of mentor competence offered a broad framework allowing for a broad assessment of mentoring skill and knowledge that may apply to undergraduate education. The model challenges assumptions that all mentoring relationships are good or that all faculty know how to mentor. Rather, he suggested that mentoring competence is based on three components: virtues, skill, and competencies. Virtues are the foundation of the triangle and of good mentoring practice, highlighting the importance of mentors having a high degree of integrity, care, and prudence. Abilities form one arm of the triangle and address the cognitive, emotional, and relational capacities that a mentor must have to fulfill their roles and responsibilities, including cognitive complexity, intellectual skills, and capacity for intimacy. Virtues and abilities make mentoring competencies possible, which are the skills demonstrated by effective mentors, making the second arm of the triangle. Competencies include knowledge about student development, self-awareness, cross-race and cross-gender engagement skills, and knowledge about mentor functions. Balance across all three arms of the triangle signifies high mentor competence and promotes more productive relationships. Johnson suggested that these components should be incorporated into faculty evaluation and training to promote more positive experiences and educational gains across developmental relationships.

Along similar lines, Larose and Tarabulsy (2005) offered the mentoring sociomotivational model, which focuses attention on mentor behaviors that facilitate student growth, development, and internal motivation. According to this framework, four sets of behaviors are critical for mentors to engage to support student outcomes. Mentors must provide structure, presenting guidelines and a plan of action. Second, they must be open to engagement, or open conversations and discussions about personal, academic, and career issues. Third, autonomy support requires allowing students to make their own choices without pressure or coercion. Finally, competence support is connected to affirmation, particularly when facing challenges.

Girves, Zepeda, and Gwathmey (2005) looked beyond individual relationships and offered a list of criteria to identify successful mentoring program offices. These criteria include administrative support, the coordination and facilitation of activities, the development of a strong pool of mentors and protégés, marketing and communication, evaluation and tracking, offering recommendations for policy and practice, and offering workshops, an orientation, and social activities.

Keller (2005) also looked beyond individual relationships, integrating a student's larger network in the systematic model of youth mentoring intervention. Keller considered the efficacy of mentoring interventions (e.g., Big Brothers/Big Sisters) and the role of a child's network in promoting or undermining pathways of information and influence. Keller argued that there are a number of relationships in a child's network. Children are placed at the center of the model, surrounded by and connected to their parents, mentors, and caseworkers. The model also includes bidirectional arrows between parents, caseworkers, and mentors, highlighting how their interactions with one another can ultimately influence interactions between the student and mentor.

Process-based frameworks also offer insight into what may motivate mentors and mentees to form these relationships. Social exchange frameworks offer a unique opportunity to consider how mentors and students make choices about how much and with whom they will interact (Johnson et al., 2007). Although working within the context of higher education requires some level of commitment to student development, social exchange suggests individuals can choose whether they will participate in relationships of greater depth or longer duration than required. According to the principles of social exchange, individuals do not act out of altruism; every relationship is based on an exchange with another party to gain access to something of value (Emerson, 1981). Although all interactions come at some kind of cost, relationships continue because they provide valued benefits (Molm, 2006). Individuals cultivate and invest resources in relationships that will yield them a significant "profit" or where the benefits of interacting will ultimately outweigh the costs

(Ensher, Thomas, & Murphy, 2001; Gibb, 1999; Homans, 1958). In the case of mentoring, relationships would be anticipated to continue when both mentors and mentees perceive themselves as giving and receiving support, resources, and opportunities for collaboration in exchange for their time and energy.

Finally, scholars have also used identity-based mentoring models to understand motivation and the desire to form and engage in mentoring relationships, speaking to how mentoring can promote social justice and equity in the academy. Research suggests both students and mentors are driven by the principle of homophily, or the tendency to build bonds and relationships with individuals perceived as similar to oneself (Bowman, Kite, Branscombe, & Williams, 1999). Homophily may explain why students of color often express a desire to engage with and form close mentoring relationships with faculty and administrators who share their racial and ethnic identities, as students seek a unique understanding of their backgrounds and experiences in higher education (Griffin, 2013). However, it is also important to note that homophily may limit the access women and men of color have to mentorship, as White and male mentors may feel more of a connection and reach out with greater frequency to White and male students.

Guiffrida (2005) offered *othermothering* as framework to understand the supportive, intrusive, advocacy-based strategies in which faculty whom Black students labeled as "student centered" engaged. Dating back to slavery, Black women have *parented* children with whom they have no biological relationship, taking responsibility for socializing and educating them as a form of community engagement and uplift. Faculty engaged in othermothering believed in students' abilities to succeed, advocated for students, maintained high expectations, and took a holistic approach to academic and career development, behaviors with which Black students largely resonated. Although othermothering is not exclusive to Black faculty, students participating in Guiffrida's study mostly identified Black faculty as exhibiting behaviors consistent with this frame, describing White faculty as helpful, but less invested, intrusive, and actively supportive.

Whereas homophily may continue to drive relationships, the increasing diversity of undergraduate education, coupled with stagnation in the representation of women and men of color in the professoriate creates conditions under which mentors and protégés are less likely to share the same identities (Girves et al., 2005). Identity-based frameworks largely address how to navigate mentoring relationships when the mentor and protégé embrace different social identities, focusing most often on race and gender. Reddick and Pritchett (2015) integrated identity and ally development in the framing of their research, advancing a cross-racial ally mentorship model based on their interviews with six White faculty members who mentor Black students. Within this model, faculty progress through stages in their development of skills and commitments to cross-racial mentoring, including an awareness of issues facing Black students, gaining access to information and educating themselves about social justice issues, adopting skills that allowed them to relate to their mentees, and empowering students to take action. This model is grounded in trust and intimacy and was linked to mentors embracing a more constant stance against discrimination and marginalization in their public lives.

Somewhat similarly, Benishek, Bieschke, Park, and Slattery (2004) offered a model that integrates a feminist model of mentoring with the principles of multiculturalism in an effort to facilitate interactions between mentors and mentees who do not share the same identities. The Multicultural Feminist model of mentoring has five dimensions that should govern mentoring relationships, intended to empower protégés and recognize identity. This model suggests that mentoring relationships should (a) rethink and challenge power structures and dynamics; (b) embrace the principles of relational mentoring, emphasizing honesty, network development, and open conversation about multicultural issues; (c) place a high value on collaboration; (d) integrate dichotomies, encouraging a congruent sense of self and validating personal experiences; and (e) incorporate a political analysis that challenges the status quo, particularly racism, sexism, classism, and heterosexism.

Outcomes-Based Frameworks

Jacobi (1991) noted the importance—and unfortunate lack of—a theoretical base that connects mentoring to academic outcomes. Jacobi highlighted four high-potential theoretical orientations that scholars could integrate into their work: (a) involvement in learning, (b) academic and social integration, (c) social support, and (d) developmental support. Few mentoring scholars appear to be using frameworks focused on social support, which emphasize how relationships reduce stress and promote coping, or developmental support, linking mentorship to the college student developmental process. There appears to be some implementation of involvement in learning-based and integration-based frameworks.

Frameworks focused on involvement in learning affirm the connection between energy invested in the educational process, retention, and success. Specifically, Astin's (1984) theory of involvement is mentioned in the framing of some mentoring research (e.g., Apprey et al., 2014; Craney et al., 2011). Astin argued that students gain more from the college experience when they are involved, investing more physical and mental effort both qualitatively and quantitatively than those students who are not as involved. Research integrating this framework has considered mentoring as a vehicle for involvement, and consequently linked to success. Frequent and high-quality interactions with faculty in educationally meaningful activities is one representation of a high level of involvement, and has been connected to students' educational gains and academic success (Astin, 1993).

Frameworks related to academic and social integration are more frequently mentioned in relation to mentoring research, most notably drawing on Tinto's (1993) model of institutional departure (e.g., Barnett, 2011; Collings, Swanson, & Watson, 2014). An emphasis on academic and social integration focuses attention on the relationship between institutional commitment, a sense of belonging and integration into the academic environment, and student persistence. Tinto's framework centers social and academic integration and suggests students who are more engaged in campus life have opportunities to develop relationships and connections, leading to academic and social integration. These students, according to the framework, are likely to feel more integrated within the campus community, and as such more likely to persist. Tinto highlighted the importance of interaction with faculty in this process, and studies applying this frame suggest a relationship between mentorship, integration, and retention.

Scholars have implemented two additional theoretical orientations in mentoring research, aiming to establish relationships between the factors of socialization and social capital and student outcomes. Socialization can be understood as the process of gaining the skills, knowledge, values, and habits associated with the society in which one is a member (Bragg, 1976; Weidman, 2006). According to Bragg, socialization captures both the cognitive and affective dimensions of learning in college, and introduction to academic norms is an important mediator for other important educational outcomes such as academic achievement, persistence, and degree completion. Weidman (1989; Weidman & Stein, 2003) noted the influence of faculty throughout the socialization process, addressing their role in engaging students in the social and academic dimensions of campus. Engaging students through the processes of advising, coaching, mentoring, the provision of constructive criticism, and collegiality allows faculty to transmit the norms and values of their institution and field of study (Bragg, 1976). Further, there is a positive relationship between the frequency and quality of interactions students have with faculty and their level of socialization (Weidman, 1989; Weidman & Stein, 2003).

Mentoring researchers are increasingly relying on social capital-based frameworks to explain the relationship between mentoring and student achievement and success, particularly emphasizing how mentoring can be a means to promote social justice (e.g., Museus & Neville, 2012; Parks-Yancy, 2012; Rios-Aguilar & Diel-Amen, 2012; Tovar, 2014). In his discussion of multiple forms of capital, Bourdieu (1986) addressed how class translates to resources that go beyond finances. Bourdieu described three kinds of capital, or accumulated labor that allows some to gain advantages over others. Social capital is most relevant to conversations about mentoring and captures social obligations, networks, and relationships that contain information and resources that can be translated to economic capital. An individual's access to social capital is not only determined by the size of their network but also their ability to mobilize the resources within it. The strength and diversity of the relationships formed facilitate important opportunities to gain access to resources.

As applied to mentoring relationships, social capital frameworks highlight how mentors are part of students' networks and can provide protégés with access to new connections. Gaining access to social capital through mentorship may be particularly important for first-generation college students (Parks-Yancy, 2012) and students of color (Museus & Neville, 2012; Rios-Aguilar & Deil-Amen, 2010; Tovar, 2014). Research suggests that both populations may have less access to information-rich networks prior to attending college, and may be excluded from such networks due to the multiple forms of marginalization they face.

Yosso (2005) offered a similar, but conceptually distinct, understanding of the resources to which students from underserved and marginalized backgrounds gain access in mentoring relationships. This perspective uses Critical Race Theory to challenge traditional notions of capital, which tend to focus on what marginalized and minoritized students do not have access to rather than their assets. Community cultural wealth recenters the experiences of students of color and the accumulated assets within their families and communities. Yosso identified six forms of wealth, which are skills, abilities, and contexts that facilitate survival and resistance in the face of challenges. Social capital is also included in the community cultural wealth framework, highlighting the importance of networks and resources that reside in students' communities. Aspirational capital represents the resources students can draw from their own and their family's sense of hope and dreams for the future, and linguistic capital is transmitted through the ability speak multiple languages or using multiple styles of communication. Navigational capital is developed as students have to navigate multiple social institutions, and resistant capital is related to observing and engaging multiple forms of protest and opposition. Finally, familial capital describes the strength that can be drawn from connections to one's family, history, and heritage. When viewed within this frame, mentoring relationships may provide students access to new forms of capital, but also help them tap into the capital they possess within their own communities (Luna & Prieto, 2009).

Finally, Hunt and Michael's (1983) research framework may be helpful in examining the relationship between mentoring and outcomes for mentors, students, and higher education institutions. Although this model does not aim to explain how or why mentoring relationships influence outcomes, it offers a framework for research and explains the factors that should be considered when engaging in mentoring research and aiming to establish a relationship between mentoring and outcomes. Hunt and Michael identify five interrelated constructs: (a) the context of the relationship, (b) mentor characteristics, (c) protégé characteristics, (d) stages of the relationship, and (e) outcomes of the relationship for the mentor, protégé, and organization. Context refers to how the cultural context within which mentoring relationships takes place may shape those relationships and student outcomes. When applied to higher education, such contexts can be the field of study, academic department, or institution. The categories of mentor characteristics and protégé characteristics call attention the potential influence of key demographic characteristics, such as race, age, and gender, as well as an individual's power and position in an organization. Finally, this model addresses the importance of considering the stage of the relationship in mentoring research, differentiating between the four relationship stages: initiation, the protégé stage, breakup, and lasting friendship.

Summary and Conclusions

The application of theory to mentoring research, training, and practice can lead to more reliable measurement and development of the positive outcomes associated with these relationships. Theory can help the field move beyond conversations that emphasize the importance of having a mentor to designing interventions that provide access to the specific aspects of mentoring relationships that can cultivate learning and development. However, this review of current research suggests that theory is inconsistently integrated into research on undergraduates' experiences and outcomes associated with mentoring. This chapter offers a way to organize and reconceptualize how theory can be used to frame mentoring research and intervention, differentiating between theories used to identify how mentoring is distinct from other relationships; the stages, phases, and quality of interactions between mentor and protégé; and how and why mentoring is related to particular student outcomes. Although there are a fair number of frameworks that aim to identify and define the components of mentoring relationships, scholarship that sheds light on how mentoring is related to student development, learning, and success is particularly limited. Further, theoretical models that integrate identity and continue to interrogate how identity can shape how mentoring is defined, how individuals engage one another, and what protégés need is also important for advancing mentoring research and practice. Attending more closely to what is happening within the context of relationships, how interactions are structured, and the behaviors most connected to specific outcomes may create opportunities to develop new frameworks explaining the important relationship between mentoring and student outcomes.

Conclusions and Recommendations

THIS FINAL CHAPTER provides a synthesis of findings presented throughout the monograph, highlighting how empirical and theoretical understanding of mentoring has advanced since the last critical review by Crisp and Cruz, published in 2009. The monograph concludes with recommendations to guide research and practice both within and outside the context of formal mentoring programs, with specific attention to how mentoring can be used to promote social justice, equity, and inclusion in higher education. We offer key recommendations for how theory and research can be used guide the development and implementation of mentoring efforts. Finally, we propose an integrated conceptual framework representing the various characteristics, experiences and outcomes empirically and theoretically related to students' developmental relationships in an effort to guide future research, program development, and the implementation of mentoring initiatives.

Synthesis of Key Findings

The reviewed studies affirm the value of both formal mentoring programs and natural mentoring relationships in supporting undergraduate students' development and success. Both formal and informal mentors can play central roles in shaping and guiding undergraduate students' college pathways. Although many of the reviewed studies had limitations, such as an absence of a control group or small nonrepresentative samples (see discussion of limitations later in this chapter), findings across qualitative and quantitative studies and diverse designs add to the growing body of evidence to suggest that mentoring programs and relationships can be an effective means to support students' adjustment to college, development, academic progress, and success. In fact, among the 109 reviewed studies, mentoring relationships were found in nearly all cases to be beneficial in some way to students and/or mentors.

The reviewed research extends prior knowledge regarding potential benefits of mentoring for both the protégé (student) and mentor (Amaral & Vala, 2009; Campbell, Smith, Dugan, & Komives, 2012), sensemaking of the mentoring relationship and associated experiences (Griffin, 2013; Luna & Prieto, 2009), and mentoring as related to civic outcomes such as social responsibility and socially responsive leadership (Haddock et al., 2013). Qualitative findings also add to knowledge regarding the mentee and mentor matching process, students' and mentors' expectations for mentoring relationships, and what mentoring looks like in the context of particular disciplines and programs. In comparison to prior reviews, we note a sizable increase in the number of published studies focused on peer-mentoring relationships. These findings have direct implications for guiding the mentoring program development and administration, as discussed later in the chapter.

Mentoring can be an effective means of promoting social justice and equity and diversity, particularly in STEM fields. A wide array of mentoring programs at community colleges and 4-year universities have been successful in increasing developmental and academic outcomes (e.g., adjustment, degree completion, and graduate school enrollment) for students from underrepresented minority populations. A few national and institution-based programs have been particularly effective in mentoring underserved groups of students and/or diversifying STEM fields, such as the National Science Foundation Research Experiences for Undergraduates (REU), Ronald E. McNair Scholars Program, the Entering Mentoring curriculum, and the Meyerhoff Scholarship Program at the University of Maryland Baltimore County. The International Mentoring Association has identified one program as top certified—an undergraduate mentoring program at Elmhurst College in Elmhurst, Illinois (http://www.elmhurst.edu/cpe/careereducation/133243108.html).

Mentoring scholars appear to be moving toward a more contextualized understanding of mentoring relationships for undergraduates. For instance, researchers have increasingly focused on how students and mentors make meaning of their mentoring experiences in ways that reflect their lived experiences. Students and mentors with different background and educational experiences (e.g., racial/ethnic group and first-generation status) may have somewhat different mentoring needs, perceptions, and experiences. The present review also revealed increased attention by scholars to identity and homophily in relationships, particularly as the student body has diversified more quickly than the faculty. We also discovered increasing attention to institutional context. Present findings also add to knowledge regarding the role of mentoring in supporting students who attend diverse institutional types including community colleges and minority serving institutions (e.g., Crisp, 2009, 2010; Perna et al., 2009; Torres Campos et al., 2009).

Likewise, mentoring researchers are moving beyond the dyadic relationship to explore the influence of mentoring at the programmatic level (Ketola, 2009). Although the benefits of mentoring relationships are not sufficiently understood, findings reveal that they may vary across programs. For example, orientation, first-year experience, and retention programs are likely to be successful in helping students adjust to college whereas undergraduate research programs may be expected to provide more opportunities for professional growth and development.

Enduring Limitations and Recommendations for Future Research

Although the mentoring literature has moved forward in some important ways since Crisp and Cruz's (2009) review, many opportunities to develop our empirical and theoretical understanding of mentoring remain. The following paragraphs parallel conceptual, methodological, and theoretical limitations of previous reviews discussed in the first chapter. In addition to identifying persistent limitations, we offer recommendations for how scholars may best respond to these limitations in future mentoring studies.

Conceptual Issues

There continues to be a lack of clarity and consistency in mentoring scholarship. Part of this challenge is rooted in the failure to establish a common definition of mentoring, despite efforts to do so. The concept of mentoring has become a big umbrella that includes all types of supportive relationships (Dawson, 2014), blurring the lines between teaching, advising, and what is called mentoring. There is also conceptual overlap between what is described as a mentoring program and the intervention being provided to students. For instance, this review identified peer mentoring programs that seem to overlap with supplemental instruction programming (e.g., Guillory, 2009; Mahlab, 2010). On the other hand, some programs incorporate mentoring, but in inconsistent ways. Many undergraduate research programs were designed to include a mentoring component with the supervising faculty member. However, in practice, the faculty member may not perceive him or herself as a mentor and the students' "mentoring" experience may not involve any support outside of the research activity. In the absence of a clear or complete conceptualization of mentoring, we suggest that researchers provide a clear definition of mentoring and distinction between it and other related program activities.

The present review highlights a need to better understand the aspects of mentoring that are most beneficial to students and mentors. Despite the growing number of studies focused on mentoring undergraduate students, we still know little about why and under which conditions mentoring is most effective. Research is needed in a few focused areas to answer this question. First, there is a need to understand how and why mentors and students are or are not able to develop meaningful connections. Relatedly, there is a need for work that identifies the specific mentoring tasks or activities that are most effective in providing various types of support and how these activities may be similar or different for different student populations (e.g., older versus younger students and active military/veteran students). Additionally, extending the work of Holt and Berwise (2012) and Behar-Horenstein, Roberts, and Dix (2010), there is a need for research to examine how different groups (e.g., students and mentors of different racial/ethnic groups) experience mentoring.

Another area of research that has yet to be fully explored is students' predispositions to mentoring. Findings by Henry et al. (2011) suggest that students' predisposition toward mentoring may influence outcomes. However, it is unclear whether or how some students are likely to benefit more from mentoring and the characteristics (e.g., first-generation status) or conditions (e.g., matching process) that might serve to influence students' predisposition toward mentoring. In the same way, there is a need to identify the mentoring roles, activities, and experiences that may yield the best outcomes. For example, is degree and career support from faculty mentors most effective in an undergraduate research experience or might it be that degree and career support is more valuable when provided by advisors or other staff? Future research must more clearly distinguish among mentoring roles and activities and their connection to the purpose of, as well as intensity of investment in, the relationship.

Moreover, future research must continue to consider the role of context in shaping the experiences and outcomes within mentoring relationships. As noted earlier, we identified relatively little research that considered the role of the institution or department in shaping mentoring experiences and outcomes. Although a few research studies were conducted at diverse institutional types such as minority serving nstitutions and programs, a much more sophisticated understanding is needed about *why* and *how* the context surrounding students serves to influence outcomes.

Methodological Issues

The present review also identified persistent methodological issues that continue to limit researchers' abilities to measure cause-and-effect relationships between mentoring and various outcomes. Mentoring is often a component of broader student success programs such as learning communities and undergraduate research programs. These programs often involve multiple interventions designed to promote student development and success (e.g., Craney et al., 2011; Deaton & Deaton, 2012; Kendricks & Arment, 2011). There are multiple challenges associated with evaluating the effectiveness of the mentoring that takes place within the context of these programs. For example, program reviews (e.g., Apprey et al., 2014; Corso & Devine, 2013; Thompson,

Jefferies, & Topping, 2010) did not typically offer a full description of the mentoring component of the program, limiting researchers' ability to understand what mentoring relationships looked like and why they were expected to positively contribute to program objectives. Also, assessments of program effectiveness are almost always limited to the program objectives, which are often not meaningfully connected to students' relationships their mentors (e.g., Dodson et al., 2009), making it difficult to draw conclusions specific to the impact and influence of mentoring. More rigorous program evaluations that offer rich descriptions of the amounts and types of mentoring provided to students and that include outcome measures that clearly connect to students' mentoring experiences are certainly warranted (for one example, see the evaluation by Torres Campos et al., 2009).

A second enduring methodological limitation in understanding the outcomes of mentoring is the lack of inclusion of control groups, which allow researchers to compare outcomes between those mentored and those who are not (Chester, Burton, Xenos, & Elgar, 2013). Failure to include a comparable control group limits the ability to determine whether outcomes could be reliably connected to students' mentoring experiences. Azic and Antulic's (2013) work suggests that there are systematic differences between students who choose and who do not choose to participate in a mentoring program. Further, the recruitment and selection processes used by mentoring programs are not always clearly described. There may be an assumption that the majority of students who participate self-select into mentoring programs and that there are systematic differences between students that may be related to program outcomes that need to be controlled for as programs are evaluated. Researchers should be sure to use control groups that have characteristics similar to those engaged in mentoring programs, such as high levels of motivation or interest in faculty interaction.

A third methodological limitation is the lack of generalizability of findings. Similar to previous reviews, we found that the large majority of studies were conducted at single institutions. The present review also revealed that most formal mentoring programs appear to be designed for a particular student population served by the institution. Although this makes practical sense and is likely to enhance benefits to program participants, the limited generalizability or replicability of programs limits researchers' abilities to draw comparisons or conclusions across programs and institutions.

Theoretical Issues

Mentoring scholars have repeatedly critiqued the state of research, noting the lack of theory as researchers attempt to clarify the scope of mentoring relationships, understand the nature of interaction, and identify why and how these relationships relate to educational and social outcomes for both mentors and protégés (e.g., Benishek et al., 2004; Johnson et al., 2007). Consistent with this critique, most research reviewed for this monograph does not incorporate a mentoring-focused theoretical framework, with the exception of unique conceptual models that are rarely translated to other research.

A closer examination of extant and emerging theory reveals that there are multiple frameworks that may provide insight into the structure, nature, and outcomes associated with mentoring. As researchers continue to wrestle with whether and how to advance a consistent definition of mentoring, it may be helpful to further develop typology-based frameworks to clarify the type and characteristics of the relationships described within one's research. Implementation of these frameworks can add some degree of consistency to mentoring research, allowing for comparisons across studies that employ similar frameworks and understandings of the definition, functions, and structure of mentoring relationships.

Further, extant theories largely focus on mentoring dyads. However, there are a few theories acknowledging the interconnectedness of relationships, highlighting how the multiple relationships in which protégés are engaged can influence one another, and the protégé's outcomes (e.g., Higgins & Kram, 2001; Keller, 2005). Greater focus on theories that explain how mentoring relationships function and the resulting outcomes when multiple actors are involved would certainly be welcome and warranted.

Mentoring scholars would also be well served to more frequently engage and develop process-based frameworks as they aim to promote both the frequency of engagement in mentoring and quality of relationships. Understanding factors that motivate mentors and protégés to engage may be particularly important, as students tend to avoid opportunities to interact with faculty beyond coursework and classroom experiences (Cotton & Wilson, 2006; Cox & Orehovec, 2007). Faculty members also may have little motivation to engage, considering that tenure and advancement systems rarely provide incentives for engagement in mentorship (Tierney & Bensimon, 1996). Studies applying social exchange frameworks (e.g., Eagan, Sharkness, Hurtado, Mosqueda, & Chang, 2011; Griffin, 2012, 2013) have found that engaging with well-trained or high-achieving students, particularly within the context of research, can increase faculty productivity, making these interactions attractive and motivating engagement. However, social exchange frameworks have rarely been applied to address student motivation to engage in mentorship. More generally, little theory focuses on understanding student motivation, instead focusing on student outcomes associated with engagement.

Theories addressing relationship quality may be helpful as researchers aim to understand the relationship between mentorship and student outcomes. Interestingly, the theoretical frameworks included in this monograph largely address the mentor's role in promoting relationship quality, addressing the skills, competencies, and values necessary to successfully engage protégés (Johnson, 2003; Larose & Tarabulsy, 2005; Reddick & Pritchett, 2015). Although similar skills and competencies may be relevant for students, given their more junior role and position as the less experienced member of the relationship, there may be a distinctive set of characteristics that make an effective protégé. Given the reciprocal nature of mentoring relationships (Kram, 1988), it would be useful to continue to explore and develop theory addressing protégé competencies and how they ultimately translate to relationship success and outcomes.

Scholars must continue to not only leverage but also develop new theoretical frameworks and conceptual models that more fully address the outcomes of mentoring relationships. Although decades of research illustrate the connections between mentoring and undergraduate educational outcomes, we perhaps continue to know least about why mentoring is related to student outcomes or how these relationships facilitate growth and development. Involvement, integration, socialization, and social capital serve as useful theoretical guides; however, frameworks within these categories are generally broad and rarely specific to mentoring relationships. Further, they may account for one

FIGURE 1
Mentoring Undergraduate Students

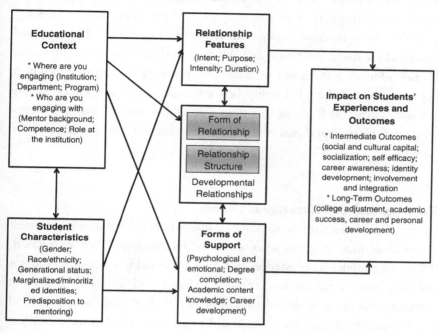

specific outcome related to mentoring, such as persistence, sense of belonging, academic achievement, or efficacy; there are no frameworks that explain why mentorship is related to a broad range of career and psychosocial outcomes. The following section draws together existing theory to offer a model that offers tentative hypotheses about how the various characteristics of mentoring may be related, to be rigorously tested by mentoring scholars moving forward.

Proposed Conceptual Framework: Mentoring Undergraduate Students

Figure 1 presents an integrated conceptual model of mentoring undergraduate students that identifies connections between developmental relationships, students' characteristics, educational context (including the institutional or programmatic context and mentor characteristics), relationship features such as intent and intensity, forms of support, and potential short- and long-term impacts on students' college experiences and outcomes. The proposed framework is based on Hunt and Michael's (1983) work and integrates theories addressing functions of mentoring relationships, forms of support they provide, and the relationship between experiences and outcomes. We also used empirical findings discussed throughout the monograph to develop and offer hypotheses about how elements of the model may be related.

Students and the Educational Context

The proposed framework is grounded by students and the educational context surrounding mentoring and other supportive relationships (Hunt & Michael, 1983). The model acknowledges the interconnectedness between students and their educational contexts. Students choose and influence their environment, and the educational environment simultaneously acts upon and shapes students, driving their needs and resources available within mentoring relationships. Undergraduate students' sociodemographic characteristics and identities, aspirations and career choice, and existing supportive relationships are thought to collectively influence students' openness and approach to a mentoring relationship (Keller, 2005). For instance, as discussed in the second chapter, findings by Mekolichick and Gibbs (2012) suggest that first-generation students may approach mentoring relationships from a more utilitarian perspective when compared to students from families with college experiences.

Within our framework, educational context includes the organizational structure within which the relationship takes place, as well as the individual with whom the student is engaging. Institutions, departments, and structured programs have distinct norms, values, and expectations about faculty–student interaction, mentorship, and developmental networks. For example, faculty at liberal arts institutions, Historically Black Colleges and Universities, and Tribal Colleges in particular may tend to be more focused on faculty–student interaction and mentorship given how their institutions prioritize teaching, learning, and student development. Mentorship appears to take place most often within the context of laboratory research in the sciences, which may require different norms and fulfill different needs than mentorship that occurs within the context, for example, of a summer bridge program.

Further, the model reminds that mentoring may involve one or many individuals or sources including faculty, staff, graduate students, peers, or external sources such as older siblings or other family members. The skills, competencies, and motivations of mentors can have great influence on developmental relationships and outcomes. The proposed framework posits that the characteristics and prior experiences mentors bring to the relationship, as well as mentors' competence and commitment to the relationship, serve to shape the effectiveness of the relationship (Johnson, 2003). The model also assumes that some sources may be more competent than others at providing various types of mentoring support. For instance, a staff member may be better suited to providing degree and career support than a peer or family member.

Relationship Features

The conceptual model proposes that both undergraduate students and the educational context influence the intent, purpose, intensity (breadth), and duration (length) of mentoring relationships (Mertz, 2004). Although often overlooked in scholarship, our model proposes that the intent of the relationship (both on the part of students and mentors) is an important feature of mentoring and other developmental relationships (Mertz & Pfleeger, 2002). It is expected that a mentoring relationship may serve one or more purposes and that the purposes of the relationship shape the choices that students and mentors make about the relationship (Johnson et al., 2007). The model further posits that not all developmental relationships require the same level of closeness or intensity (Rusbult, 1983) and that mentoring relationships may be separated by the intensity or duration of the relationship.

Forms of Support

The conceptual model proposes that students may receive one or more of the following overlapping forms of support from mentors or other supportive relationships: (a) psychological and emotional support such as interacting in an authentic and caring manner, encouraging, motivating students, relating to their worldview, affirming, and befriending; (b) degree completion support such as advising, providing feedback, and helping students navigate academic policy and degree requirements; (c) academic subject knowledge support such as teaching, sharing information, involving students in research, and creating awareness of resources; and (d) career development support such as networking, internships and apprenticeships, career goal and aspiration setting, and role modeling (Crisp, 2009; Kram, 1988; Nora & Crisp, 2007). The educational context is assumed to influence the types of support provided to students, as well as students' needs. At the same time, the proposed model posits that students' characteristics influence the types of mentoring support students need.

Types of Developmental Relationships

Relationship features and forms of support converge to shape and define developmental relationships, which serve as a vehicle for receipt of support and guidance. Although emphasis may be placed on whether or not students have access to mentoring, this framework highlights how forms of support offered within the context of a relationship and relationship features can be used to define and distinguish relationships from one another. Further, it reminds us that relationship functions and features are the drivers of student outcomes, rather simply having access to specific kinds of relationships.

First, the conceptual model distinguishes between different forms of developmental or supportive relationships (Johnson, 2015). Not all supportive relationships should be classified as mentoring and take various forms which may both overlap and be distinct in terms of intent, purpose, intensity, and duration including advisors, guides, counselors, developers, role models, and mentors (Kram, 1985). For example, Baker and Griffin (2010) suggested that advising relationships may be focused on academic subject knowledge and degree-related support and of less intensity and shorter duration than mentoring relationships, which more often incorporate psychological and emotional support as well as career support. At the same time, forms of relationships can and often do change with time; for instance, advisors can develop into mentors. Second, the model acknowledges the importance of mentoring structure. For example, an e-mentoring relationship may fulfill different functions and have a different intent and duration than face-to-face advising, which may also be distinct from naturally forming mentoring relationships. Similarly, group mentoring may create opportunities to offer unique forms of support unavailable through one-on-one relationships.

Impact on Students' Experiences and Outcomes

Although not well understood, the framework assumes that different types and forms of support have both overlapping and distinct benefits or impacts on undergraduate students. The influence and outcomes of mentoring support are assumed to be conditionally dependent on the features of the mentoring relationship (e.g., purpose and intensity). Drawing from empirical findings and theory presented throughout this monograph, the proposed model hypothesizes that mentoring can have a direct, positive impact on various student outcomes, such as career development and academic achievement or degree attainment. Mentoring may also have an indirect influence on long-term outcomes through its relationship with intermediate outcomes, defined as outcomes that are a direct result of experiences in the college environment (Astin, 1993), including (a) increasing social and cultural capital (Bourdieu, 1986), (b) socialization to the college environment (Bragg, 1976; Weidman, 1989), (c) involvement and integration (Astin, 1984; Tinto, 1993), (d) self-efficacy, (e) career awareness, (f) civic awareness, and (g) identity development. Engagement, or energy invested in campus life academically and socially, is one example of an important intermediate outcome linked to important, longer term educational outcomes (Astin, 1993) such as college adjustment, career and personal development, and academic progress and success. For example, students who develop supportive relationships with faculty are likely to become more integrated into the academic and social life of their institutions, which in turn may make them more likely to persist in college (Tinto, 1993). Similarly, socialization, or learning the norms and values of one's institution or field, can be fostered in mentoring relationships and is assumed to lead to academic achievement, persistence, and degree completion (Bragg, 1976).

Evidence-Based Mentoring Practices

We conclude with a discussion of how these findings may be directly applied to the development, implementation, and evaluation of formal mentoring programs. We identify evidence-based practices as well as exemplary mentoring programs that may serve as models for program design.

Identifying Mentors

The development of a strong pool of mentors and protégés is critical to the success of formal mentoring programs (Girves et al., 2005). The present review identified several evidence-based practices for identifying mentors. Empirical evidence suggests that when possible, programs should use an individualized process for selecting mentors (Bell & Treleaven, 2010). Potential mentors should be encouraged to be honest with themselves about the time and commitment they have to offer to a mentoring relationship (Baker & Griffin, 2010). Present findings also suggest that we must look beyond faculty as student mentors; various individuals can serve as effective mentors for undergraduate students, including peers, graduate students, staff, and faculty. At the same time, it is important to distinguish between individuals who are expected to serve as mentors from those who may provide related forms of support. For example, an academic advisor often focuses on offering instrumental academic support and guidance toward degree completion and may or may not serve as a mentor to an undergraduate student by integrating emotional support or demonstrating a different level of intent, intensity, and duration in the context of the relationship.

Findings also reveal the importance of matching beyond a student's subject area. Students' and mentors' prior experiences and identities are also important, and should not be ignored when matching students with mentors. Students from underrepresented or underserved backgrounds often express an interest in forming mentoring relationships with mentors who share their identities, assuming they will be able to understand and affirm their sometimes-marginalizing experiences in the academy (Griffin, 2013; Guiffrida, 2005; Patton, 2009). At the same time, it is important to note that mentors do not necessarily have to share students' race, gender, or other personal characteristics to be effective. In fact, study findings reveal that mentoring a student who identifies as a racial/ethnic minority may benefit the mentor by developing their awareness of the challenges facing these students and/or relating to students' worldview and context (e.g., Reddick & Pritchett, 2015; Ward et al., 2014). Ultimately, what may be most important in promoting social justice through mentoring is that mentors affirm students' identities, validate their experiences and perspectives, and acknowledge how identity may relate to student persistence and success (Benishek et al., 2004; Reddick & Pritchett, 2015).

Designing Program Activities

The findings of this monograph also offer practical implications for designing mentoring program activities. When designing a mentoring program, faculty and staff should consider building in the following interrelated forms of support into the mentoring relationship: (a) psychological and emotional support; (b) degree and career support; (c) academic subject knowledge support; and (d) the presence of a role model (Crisp, 2009). Although the activities that are used to provide these forms of support will vary according to the goals and structure of the program, findings offer ideas for activities that may be effective. For instance, taking students to conferences or involving them in research may be an effective means of providing support for students in deciding on a major or career (Lunsford, 2011). Similarly, encouraging students to be aware of and connected to campus resources such as tutoring programs and clubs or organizations that reflect academic subject knowledge may foster academic achievement and strengthen connections to the campus community.

At the same time, findings suggest that students may have different needs and motivations for seeking access to mentoring relationships (Lunsford,

2011). Individual students may value different activities and forms of support (Cox, Yang, & Dicke-Bohmann, 2014). This diversity should be taken into consideration in designing mentoring activities. For example, students who are not the first in their family to attend college may expect a more personal and professional mentoring experience as compared to first-generation students, who may view and potentially gain more from a relationship that uses a more utilitarian approach (Mekolichick & Gibbs, 2012). Given their underrepresentation in the field, women students in science may be more appreciative of access to role models who share their gender identity than male students, or women in more gender-balanced or female-dominant fields. As such, consideration should be given whenever possible to the values and needs of both mentors and students as program activities are developed, taking care to understand the unique needs of the students being served (Kram, 1988).

Mentor Training

Mentor training is important to the success of mentoring relationships, particularly given the complexities in their process and development. Training can enhance mentors' competence, and thus relationship quality. For instance, a training program focused on STEM undergraduate students found that trained mentors were more likely to consider issues of diversity, discuss expectations with their undergraduate students, and discuss mentoring with other faculty and peers when compared to untrained mentors (Pfund, Pribbenow, Branchaw, Lauffer, & Handelsman, 2006). Present findings highlight several characteristics of effective mentoring relationships that may be incorporated, as appropriate, into training programs (Baker & Griffin, 2010; O'Meara, Knudsen, & Jones, 2013; Poteat, Shockley, & Allen, 2009; Shanahan, Ackley-Holbrook, Stewart, & Walkington, 2015; Straus, Johnson, Marquez, & Feldman, 2013). Those characteristics include a mentor who:

- Is willing to engage an emotional commitment to the student
- Serves as an advocate for the student
- Provides encouragement
- Motivates the student

- Sets high expectations with needed support
- Relates to the student on their level
- Demonstrates personal connection and interest in the relationship

Additionally, successful relationships are built upon clear expectations of both students and mentors, and mutual respect. Programs would be well served to consider how they are introducing students to the idea of mentoring. Training, guidance, and guidelines that allow students to articulate and assess their expectations, identify their needs, and acknowledge their role in relationship maintenance may also foster satisfaction with the quality and outcomes associated with mentoring.

Evaluating Mentoring Programs

Evaluation of mentoring programs is critically important. Although much can be learned from extant program evaluations, continued research is needed to more fully understand the relationship between mentoring, specific forms of support, and outcomes. The findings presented in this monograph also bring attention to the need to better understand relationships between program supports, activities, and outcomes. As such, we strongly recommend that evaluators not only assess overall program effectiveness but also measure impacts of specific program activities. Further, present findings reveal that mentors' and students' perceptions of the mentoring experience may not always align (e.g., Holt & Berwise, 2012). As such, it is important to gather information from both students and mentors that goes beyond simple satisfaction surveys and also includes measure of relationship quality. Despite a focus on how mentoring relationships foster student outcomes, it is also important to assess the benefits of the relationship to the mentors whenever possible. Finally, to enhance generalizability and transferability of findings, it is important to provide a clear definition and description of the mentoring relationship and activities when writing up and publishing evaluations. Such clarity can promote opportunities for comparison across studies and offer a clearer roadmap for the replication of best practices.

Concluding Remarks

Mentors and mentoring relationships continue to be widely celebrated and linked to success, both within and outside of the context of higher education. As scholars, policymakers, and institutional leaders aim to promote enhanced engagement in these relationships, it is important to understand how extant theory and research can inform mentoring practice in undergraduate education. This review of recent scholarship is intended to advance conversations about mentoring relationships and the development of data-driven practice, thereby enhancing relationship quality and outcomes for mentors and protégés. We offer these recommendations to support the faculty and staff directly involved with formal programming efforts, institutional agents who seek to engage undergraduate students in natural mentoring relationships, and researchers who continue to study the structure, characteristics, and outcomes of mentoring programs and relationships.

Rather than offering a specific series of recommendations or best practices, this volume offers new ways to think critically about mentoring research and practice. The proposed conceptual model offers a way to categorize the various factors and forces that can influence mentoring relationships and outcomes, particularly attending how the identities and needs of students and the contexts within which relationships take place influence their structures and outcomes. Although the field continues to be challenged by a lack of consistency in conceptualizing mentoring and how it differs from other relationships, the scholarship and emergent theory provide ways to understand and define mentoring within institutional contexts and student needs.

Enhancing the ability to foster positive outcomes through mentoring relationships is particularly important as higher education strives to promote equity and social justice in students' educational experiences and outcomes. Mentoring provides access to resources and experiences that are beneficial across student background and identity; however, questions remain regarding whether underrepresented and underserved students in higher education have equal access to mentors and interactions that can provide crucial support, information, and guidance. The current state of research offers a more sophisticated understanding of the potential of mentoring to support social justice/equity in higher education, moving beyond recognition of the benefits of identity homophily to acknowledging the sources of capital that are cultivated and transferred through mentoring experiences, and offering strategies for mentors to affirm students' identities and experiences.

Ultimately, mentoring in all its forms is an effort toward communicating to college students from all backgrounds that they belong, are supported, and are capable of being successful within and beyond the postsecondary environment. It is to that end that we offer this synthesis and analysis.

References

Amaral, K. E., & Vala, M. (2009). What teaching teaches: Mentoring and the performance gains of mentors. *Chemical Education Research, 86*(5), 629–633.

Anderson, E. M., & Shannon, A. L. (1988). Toward a conceptualization of mentoring. *Journal of Teacher Education, 39*, 38–42.

Anderson, M., Lyons, K., & Weiner, N. (2014). *The honors thesis: A handbook for honors deans, directors, and faculty advisors.* Lincoln, NE: National Collegiate Honors Council.

Apprey, M., Preston-Grimes, P., Bassett, K. C., Lewis, D. W., & Rideau, R. M. (2014). From crisis management to academic achievement: A university cluster-mentoring model for Black undergraduates. *Peabody Journal of Education, 89*(3), 318–335. doi: 10.1080/0161956X.2014.913446

Astin, A. W. (1984). Student involvement: A developmental theory for higher education. *Journal of College Student Personnel, 22*, 297–308.

Astin, A. W. (1993). *What matters in college?: Four critical years revisited.* San Francisco, CA: Jossey-Bass.

Azic, S. S., & Antulic, S. (2013). Adjustment to college and the student mentoring programme. *Croatian Journal of Education, 15*(3), 715–740.

Baker, V. L. (2016). Undergraduate research as a pedagogical tool in business education: The lesson of "doing well and doing good." Perspectives on Undergraduate Research and Mentoring (PURM), Issue 5.1. Retrieved from http://blogs.elon.edu/purm/files/2016/09/Baker-et-al-PURM-5.1.pdf

Baker, V. L., & Griffin, K. A. (2010). Beyond mentoring and advising: Toward understanding the role of faculty "developers" in student success. *About Campus,* 2–8. doi: 10.1002/abc.20002

Baker, V. L., Pifer, M. J., Lunsford, L. G., Greer, J., & Ihas, D. (2015). Faculty as mentors in undergraduate research, scholarship, and creative work: Motivating and inhibiting factors. *Mentoring & Tutoring: Partnership in Learning, 23*(5), 394–410.

Barnett, E. A. (2011). Validation experiences and persistence among community college students. *Review of Higher Education, 34*(2), 193–230. doi:10.1353/rhe.2010.0019

Bean, J., & Eaton, S. B. (2001). The psychology underlying successful retention practices. *Journal of College Student Retention: Research, Theory & Practice, 3*(1), 73–89.

Beckman, M., & Hensel, N. (2009). Making explicit the implicit: Defining undergraduate research. *CUR Quarterly, 29*(4), 40–44.

Behar-Horenstein, L. S., Roberts, K. W., & Dix, A. C. (2010). Mentoring undergraduate researchers: An exploratory study of students' and professors' perceptions. *Mentoring & Tutoring: Partnership in Learning, 18*(3), 269–291. doi:10.1080/13611267.2010.492945

Bell, A., & Treleaven, L. (2010). Looking for professor right: Mentee selection of mentors in a formal mentoring program. *Higher Education, 2011*(61), 545–561. doi:10.1007/s10734-010-9348-0

Benishek, L. A., Bieschke, K. J., Park, J., & Slattery, S. M. (2004). A multicultural feminist model of mentoring. *Journal of Multicultural Counseling and Development, 32*, 428–442.

Bettinger, E., & Baker, R. (2011). *The effects of student coaching in college: An evaluation of a randomized experiment in student mentoring (Working Paper 16881).* Cambridge, MA: National Bureau of Economic Research Retrieved from http://www.nber.org/papers/w16881

Blackwell, J. E. (1989). Mentoring: An action strategy for increasing minority faculty. *Academe, 75*, 8–14.

Bordes-Edgar, V., Arredondo, P., Kurpius, S. R., & Rund, J. (2011). A longitudinal analysis of Latina/o students' academic persistence. *Journal of Hispanic Higher Education, 10*(4), 358–368. doi:10.1177/1538192711423318

Bourdieu, P. (1986). The forms of capital. In J. Richardson (Ed.), *Handbook of theory and research for the sociology of education* (pp. 241–258). Westport, CT: Greenwood.

Bower, G. G., & Bonnett, S. (2009). The examination of a mentoring relationship during a metadiscrete physical education field experience. *Journal of Research, 4*(2), 19–25.

Bowman, S. R., Kite, M. E., Branscombe, N. R., & Williams, S. (1999). Developmental relationships of Black Americans in the academy. In A. J. Murrell, F. J. Crosby, & R. J. Ely (Eds.), *Mentoring dilemmas: Developmental relationships within multicultural organizations* (pp. 21–46). Mahwah, NJ: Lawrence Erlbaum Associates.

Bragg, A. K. (1976). *The socialization process in higher education.* Washington, DC: American Association for Higher Education.

Brittian, A. S., Sy, S. R., & Stokes, J. E. (2009). Mentoring: Implications for African American college students. *Western Journal of Black Studies, 33*(2), 87.

Bruce, M., & Bridgeland, J. (2014). The mentoring effect: Young people's perspectives on the outcomes and availability of mentoring. MENTOR: The National Mentoring Partnership. Retrieved from: http://www.mentoring.org/images/uploads/Report_TheMentoring Effect.pdf

Budny, D., Paul, C. A., & Newborg, B. B. (2010). Impact of peer mentoring on freshmen engineering students. *Journal of STEM Education: Innovations and Research, 11*(5/6), 9–24.

Cambridge-Williams, T., Winsler, A., Kitsantas, A., & Bernard, E. (2013). University 100 orientation courses and living–learning communities boost academic retention and graduation via enhanced self-efficacy and self-regulated learning. *Journal of College Student Retention: Research, Theory & Practice, 15*(2), 243–268.

Campbell, C. M., Smith, M., Dugan, J. P., & Komives, S. R. (2012). Mentors and college student leadership outcomes: The importance of position and process. *Review of Higher Education, 35*(4), 595–625. doi:10.1353/rhe.2012.0037

Carter, F. D., Mandell, M., & Maton, K. I. (2009). The influence of on-campus, academic year undergraduate research on STEM Ph.D. outcomes: Evidence from the Meyerhoff Scholarship Program. *Educational Evaluation and Policy Analysis, 31*(4), 441–462.

Chemers, M. M., Zurbriggen, E. L., Syed, M., Goza, B. K., & Bearman, S. (2011). The role of efficacy and identity in science career commitment among underrepresented minority students. *Journal of Social Issues, 67*(3), 469–491.

Chester, A., Burton, L J., Xenos, S., & Elgar, K. (2013). Peer mentoring: Supporting successful transition for first year undergraduate psychology students. *Australian Journal of Psychology, 65*, 30–37. doi:0.1111/ajpy.12006

Chou, P. (2012). The integration of Facebook into class management: An exploratory study. *Educational Research, 3*(7), 572–575.

Cole, D., & Espinoza, A. (2008). Examining the academic success of Latino students in science technology engineering and mathematics (STEM) majors. *Journal of College Student Development, 49*(4), 285–300.

Cole, D., & Griffin, K. A. (2013). Advancing the study of student–faculty interaction: A focus on diverse students and faculty. In M.B. Paulsen (Ed.), *Higher education: Handbook of theory and research* (Vol. *28*, pp. 561–611). Netherlands: Springer.

Collings, R., Swanson, V., & Watkins, R. (2014). The impact of peer mentoring on levels of student wellbeing, integration and retention: A controlled comparative evaluation of residential students in UK higher education. *Higher Education, 2014*(68), 927–942. doi:10.1007/s10734-014-9752-y

Corso, J., & Devine, J. (Fall, 2013). Student technology mentors: A community college success story. *Community College Enterprise*, 9–21.

Cotton, S. R., & Wilson, B. (2006). Student–faculty interactions: Dynamics and determinants. *Higher Education, 51*, 487–519. doi:10.1007/s10734-004-1705-4

Cox, B. E., & Orehovec, E. (2007). Faculty–student interaction outside the classroom: A typology from a residential college. *The Review of Higher Education, 30*, 343–362.

Cox, C. B., Yang, Y., & Dicke-Bohmann, A. K. (2014). What do Hispanic students want in a mentor? A model of protégé cultural orientation, mentorship, expectations and performance. *Journal of Hispanic Higher Education, 13*(4), 359–376.

Craney, C., McKay, T., Mazzeo, A., & Morris, J. (2011). Cross-discipline perceptions of the undergraduate research experience. *Journal of Higher Education, 82*(1), 92–113. doi:10.1353/jhe.2011.0000

Crisp, G. (2009). Conceptualization and initial validation of the College Student Mentoring Scale (CSMS). *Journal of College Student Development, 50*(2), 177–194. doi:10.1353/csd.0.0061

Crisp, G. (2010). The impact of mentoring on the success of community college students. *Review of Higher Education, 34*(1), 39–60. doi:10.1353/rhe.2010.0003

Crisp, G. (2011). The impact of mentoring on the persistence decisions of undergraduate students attending a Hispanic Serving Institution. *Enrollment Management Journal: Student Access, Finance and Success in Higher Education, 5*(1), 32–57.

Crisp, G., & Cruz, I. (2009). Mentoring college students: A critical review of the literature between 1990 and 2007. *Research in Higher Education, 50*(6), 525–545. doi:10.1007/s11162-009-9130-2

Crisp, G., & Cruz, I. (2010). Confirmatory factor analysis of a measure of "mentoring" among undergraduate students attending a Hispanic Serving Institution. *Journal of Hispanic Higher Education, 9*(3), 232–244. doi:10.1177/1538192710371982

D'Abate, C. P. (2009). Defining mentoring in the first-year experience: One institution's approach to clarifying the meaning of mentoring first-year students. *Journal of the First-Year Experience and Students in Transition, 21*(1), 65–91.

Dahlvig, J. (2010). Mentoring of African American students at a Predominantly White Institution (PWI). *Christian Higher Education, 9*, 369–395. doi:10.1080/15363750903404266

Dawson, P. (2014). Beyond a definition: Toward a framework for designing and specifying mentoring models. *Educational Researcher, 43*(3), 137–145.

Davis, D. J. (2010). The academic influence of mentoring upon African American undergraduate aspirants to the professoriate. *Urban Review, 2010*(42), 143–158. doi:10.1007/s11256-009-0122-5

Deaton, C. C., & Deaton, B. (2012). Using mentoring to foster professional development among undergraduate instructional leaders. *Journal of College Science Teaching, 42*(1), 58–62.

DeFreitas, S. C., & Bravo, A. (2012). The influence of involvement with faculty and mentoring on the self-efficacy and academic achievement of African American and Latino college students. *Journal of the Scholarship of Teaching and Learning, 12*(4), 1–11.

Dennis, J. M., Phinney, J. S., & Chuateco, L. I. (2005). The role of motivation, parental support, and peer support in the academic success of ethnic minority first-generation college students. *Journal of College Student Development, 46*(3), 223–236. doi:10.1353/csd.2005.0023

Dodson, J. E., Montgomery, B. L., & Brown, L. J. (2009). "Take the fifth": Mentoring students whose cultural communities were not historically structured into U.S. higher education. *Innovative Higher Education, 34*, 185–199. doi:10.1007/s10755-009-9099-y

Dolan, E., & Johnson, D. (2009). Toward a holistic view of undergraduate research experiences: An exploratory study of impact on graduate/postdoctoral mentors. *Journal of Educational Technology, 18*, 487–500. doi:10.1007/s10956-009-9165-3

Dugan, J. P., & Komives, S. R. (2010). Influences on college students' capacities for socially responsible leadership. *Journal of College Student Development, 51*(5), 525–549. doi:10.1353/csd.2010.0009

Dunstan, S. B., & Jaeger, A. J. (2015). Dialect and influences on the academic experiences of college students. *Journal of Higher Education, 86*(5), 777–803.

Eagan, M. K., Jr., Sharkness, J., Hurtado, S., Mosqueda, C. M., & Chang, M. J. (2011). Engaging undergraduates in science research: Not just about faculty willingness. *Research in Higher Education, 52*(2), 151–177.

Edgcomb, M. R., Crowe, H. A., Rice, J. D., Morris, S. J., Wolffe, R. J., & McConnaughay, K. D. (2010). *Peer and near-peer mentoring: Enhancing learning in undergraduate research programs.* Washington, DC: Council on Undergraduate Research. Retrieved from www.cur.org/assets/1/7/Edgcomb.pdf

Emerson, R. M. (1981). Social exchange theory. In M. Rosenberg & R. H. Turner (Eds.), *Social psychology: Sociological perspectives* (pp. 30–65). New York, NY: Basic Books.

Ensher, E. A., Thomas, C., & Murphy, S. E. (2001). Comparison of traditional, step-ahead, and peer mentoring on protégés' support, satisfaction, and perceptions of career success: A social exchange perspective. *Journal of Business and Psychology, 15*, 419–438.

Espinoza, P. P., & Espinoza, C. C. (2012). Supporting the 7th-year undergraduate: Responsive leadership at a Hispanic Serving Institution. *Journal of Cases in Educational Leadership, 15*(1), 32–50. doi:10.1177/1555458912440738

Evans, S. D., & Prilleltensky, I. (2007). Youth and democracy: Participation for personal, relational, and collective well-being. *Journal of Community Psychology, 35*(6), 681–692.

Fechheimer, M., Webber, K., & Kleiber, P. B. (2011). How well do undergraduate research programs promote engagement and success of students? *CBE-Life Sciences Education, 10*(2), 156–163.

Fox, A., Stevenson, L., Connelly, P., Duff, A., & Dunlop, A. (2010). Peer-mentoring undergraduate accounting students: The influence on approaches to learning and academic performance. *Active Learning in Higher Education, 11*(2), 145–156. doi:10.1177/1469787410365650

Fuentes, M. V., Alvarado, A. R., Berdan, J., & DeAngelo, L. (2014). Mentorship matters: Does early faculty contact lead to quality faculty interaction? *Research in Higher Education, 55*, 288–307. doi:10.1007/s11162-013-9307-6

Gershenfeld, S. (2014). A review of undergraduate mentoring programs. *Review of Educational Research, 84*(3), 365–391. doi:10.3102/0034654313520512

Gibb, S. (1999). The usefulness of theory: A case study in evaluating formal mentoring schemes. *Human Relations, 52*(8), 1055–1075.

Girves, J. E., Zepeda, Y., & Gwathmey, J. K. (2005). Mentoring in a post-affirmative action world. *Journal of Social Issues, 61*(3), 449–479.

Goff, L. (2011). Evaluating the outcomes of a peer-mentoring program for students transitioning to postsecondary education. *The Canadian Journal for the Scholarship of Teaching and Learning, 2*(2), 2. doi: http://dx.doi.org/10.5206/cjsotl-rcacea.2011.2.2

Griffin, K. A. (2012). Black professors managing mentorship: Implications of applying social exchange frameworks to our understanding of the influence of student interaction on scholarly productivity. *Teachers College Record, 114*(5), 1–37.

Griffin, K. A. (2013). Voices of the "othermothers": Reconsidering Black professors' relationships with Black students as a form of social exchange. *Journal of Negro Education, 82*(2), 169–183.

Griffin, K. A., & Reddick, R. J. (2011). Surveillance and sacrifice: Gender differences in the mentoring patterns of Black professors at Predominantly White research universities. *American Educational Research Journal, 48*(5), 1032–1057.

Gross, D., Iverson, E., Willett, G., & Manduca, C. (2015). Research and teaching: Broadening access to science with support for the whole student in a residential liberal arts college environment. *Journal of College Science Teaching, 44*(4), n4.

Guiffrida, D. A. (2005). Othermothering as a framework for understanding African American students' definitions of student-centered faculty. *Journal of Higher Education, 76*(6), 701–723.

Guillory, R. M. (2009). American Indian/Alaska Native college student retention strategies. *Journal of Developmental Education, 3*(2), 12–38.

Haddock, S., Weiler, L. M., Krafchick, J., Zimmerman, T. S., McLure, M., & Rudisill, S. (2013). Campus corps therapeutic mentoring: Making a difference for mentors. *Journal of Higher Education Outreach and Engagement, 17*(4), 225–256.

Hébert, T. P., & McBee, M. T. (2007). The impact of an undergraduate honors program on gifted university students. *Gifted Child Quarterly, 51*(2), 136–151.

Henry, J., Bruland, H., & Sano-Franchini, J. (2011). Course-embedded mentoring for first-year students: Melding academic subject support with role modeling, psycho-social support, and goal setting. *International Journal for the Scholarship of Teaching and Learning, 5*(2), 1–22.

Higgins, M. C., & Kram, K. E. (2001). Reconceptualizing mentoring at work: A developmental network perspective. *Academic of Management Review, 26*(2), 264–288.

Higher Education Research Institute. (1996). *A social change model of leadership development (Version III)*. Los Angeles: University of California Los Angeles, Higher Education Research Institute.

Holland, J. M., Major, D. A., & Orvis, K. A. (2012). Understanding how peer mentoring and capitalization link STEM students to their majors. *Career Development Quarterly, 60*, 343–354.

Holt, L. J., & Berwise, C. A. (2012). Illuminating the process of peer mentoring: An examination and comparison of peer mentors' and first-year students' experiences. *Journal of the First-Year Experience and Students in Transition, 24*(1), 19–43.

Homans, G. C. (1958). Social behavior as exchange. *American Journal of Sociology, 63*(6), 597–606.

Hryciw, D. H., Tangalakis, K., Supple, B., & Best, G. (2013). Evaluation of a peer mentoring program for a mature cohort of first-year undergraduate paramedic students. *Advances in Physiology Education, 37*, 80–84. doi:10.1152/advan.00129.2012

Hu, S., & Ma, Y. (2010). Mentoring and student persistence in college: A study of the Washington State Achievers Program. *Innovative Higher Education, 35*(5), 329–341. doi:10.1007/s10755-010-9147-7

Hunt, D. M., & Michael, C. (1983). Mentorship: A career training and development tool. *Academy of Management Review, 8*(3), 475–485.

Hunter, A. B., Laursen, S. L., & Seymour, E. (2007). Becoming a scientist: The role of undergraduate research in students' cognitive, personal, and professional development. *Science Education, 91*(1), 36–74.

Hurtado, S., Eagan, M. K., Cabrera, N. L., Lin, M. H., Park, J., & Lopez, M. (2008). Training future scientists: Predicting first-year minority student participation in health science research. *Research in Higher Education, 49*(2), 126–152.

Inkelas, K. K., Daver, Z. E., Vogt, K. E., & Leonard, J. B. (2007). Living–learning programs and first-generation college students' academic and social transition to college. *Research in Higher Education, 48*(4), 403–434.

Inkelas, K. K., & Soldner, M. (2011). Undergraduate living–learning programs and student outcomes. In J. C. Smart & M. B. Paulsen (Eds.), *Higher education: Handbook of theory and research* (Vol. 26, pp. 1–55). New York, NY: Springer.

Ishiyama, J. (2007). Expectations and perceptions of undergraduate research mentoring: Comparing first generation, low income white/Caucasian and African American students. *College Student Journal, 41*(3), 540–549.

Jacobi, M. (1991). Mentoring and undergraduate academic success: A literature review. *Review of Educational Research, 61*(4), 505–532.

Johnson, C. S. (1989). Mentoring programs. In M. L. Upcraft, J. N. Gardner, & Associates, *The Freshman Year Experience* (pp. 118–128). San Francisco, CA: Jossey-Bass.

Johnson, B. J., Rose, G., & Schlosser, L. Z. (2007). Student–faculty mentoring: Theoretical and methodological issues. In T. D. Allen & L. T. Eby (Eds.), *The Blackwell handbook of mentoring: A multiple perspectives approach* (pp. 49–69). Malden, MA: Wiley–Blackwell.

Johnson, W. B. (2003). A framework for conceptualizing competence to mentor. *Ethics & Behavior, 13*(2), 127–151.

Johnson, W. B. (2015). On being a mentor: A guide for higher education faculty. New York, NY: Routledge.

Jokelainen, M., Turunen, H., Tossavainen, K., Jamookeeah, D., & Coco, K. (2011). A systematic review of mentoring nursing students in clinical placements. *Journal of Clinical Nursing, 20*, 2854–2867. doi:10.1111/j.1365-2702.2010.03571.x

Keller, T. E. (2005). A systemic model of the youth mentoring intervention. *Journal of Primary Prevention, 26*(2), 169–188.

Kena, G., Hussar, W., McFarland, J., de Brey, C., Musu-Gillette, L., Wang, X., …Dunlop Velez, E. (2016). *Condition of education 2016*. Washington, DC: National Center for Educational Statistics.

Kendricks, K., & Arment, A. (2011). Adopting a K–12 family model with undergraduate research to enhance STEM persistence and achievement in underrepresented minority students. *Journal of College Science Teaching, 41*(2), 22–27.

Kendricks, K. D., Nedunuri, K. V., & Arment, A. R. (2013). Minority student perceptions of the impact of mentoring to enhance academic performance in STEM disciplines. *Journal of STEM Education, 14*(2), 38–46.

Ketola, J. (2009). An analysis of a mentoring program for baccalaureate nursing students: Does the past still influence the present? *Nursing Forum, 44*(4), 245–255.

Khazanov, L. (2011). Mentoring at-risk students in a remedial mathematics course. *Mathematics and Computer Education, 106*–118.

Kift, S. (2009). *Articulating a transition pedagogy to scaffold and to enhance the first year student learning experience in Australian higher education: Final report for ALTC senior fellowship program*. Strawberry Hills, NSW: Australian Learning and Teaching Council. Retrieved from http://sydney.edu.au/education-portfolio/ei/projects/transition/ALTC%20Senior%20 Fellowship%20Report.pdf

Kim, Y. K., & Sax, L. J. (2009). Student–faculty interaction in research universities: Differences by student gender, race, social class, and first-generation status. *Research in Higher Education, 50*(5), 437–459.

Kinkel, D. H. (2011). Engaging students in career planning and preparation through e-mentoring. *Journal of Natural Resources and Life Sciences Education, 40*(1), 150–159.

Komarraju, M., Musulkin, S., & Bhattacharya, G. (2010). Role of student–faculty interactions in developing college students' academic self-concept, motivation, and achievement. *Journal of College Student Development, 51*(3), 332–342.

Kostovich, C. T., & Thurn, K. E. (2013). Group mentoring: A story of transition for undergraduate baccalaureate nursing students. *Nurse Education Today, 33*, 413–418.

Kram, K. (1985). *Mentoring at work*. Glenview, IL: Scott, Foresman.

Kram, K. E. (1988). *Mentoring at work: Developmental relationships in organizational life.* Lanham, MD: University Press of America.

Kuh, G. D., Kinzie, J., Schuh, J. H., & Whitt, E. J. (2011). *Student Success in College: Creating Conditions that Matter.* San Francisco, CA: Jossey-Bass.

Larose, S., Cyrenne, D., Garceau, O., Harvey, M., Guay, F., & Deschenes, C. (2009). Personal and support factors involved in students' decision to participate in formal academic mentoring. *Journal of Vocational Behavior, 74,* 108–116.

Larose, S., & Tarabulsy, G. M. (2005). Academically at-risk students. In D. L. DuBois & M. J. Karcher (Eds.), *Handbook of youth mentoring* (pp. 440–453). Thousand Oaks, CA: Sage.

Lopatto, D. (2007). Undergraduate research experiences support science career decisions and active learning. *CBE-Life Sciences Education, 6,* 297–306. doi:10.1187/cbe.07-06-0039

Lotkowski, V. A., Robbins, S. B., & Noeth, R. J. (2004). The role of academic and nonacademic factors in improving college retention. *ACT Policy Report.* Iowa City, IA: ACT Inc.

Luna, V., & Prieto, L. (2009). Mentoring affirmations and interventions: A bridge to graduate school for Latina/o students. *Journal of Hispanic Higher Education, 8*(2), 213–224. doi:10.1177/1538192709331972

Lunsford, L. G. (2011). Psychology of mentoring: The case of talented college students. *Journal of Advanced Academics, 22*(3), 474–498.

Lunsford, L. G. (2016). *Handbook of managing mentoring programs: Starting, supporting, and sustaining mentoring.* New York, NY: Gower.

Mahlab, M. (2010). Who benefits? Peer mentors at Grinnell College. *Council on Undergraduate Research, 31*(2), 1–7.

McNair Scholars. (n.d.) About. Retrieved from http://mcnairscholars.com/about/

Mekolichick, J., & Gibbs, M. K. (2012). *Understanding college generational status in the undergraduate research mentored relationship.* Washington, DC: Council on Undergraduate Research. Retrieved from www.cur.org/assets/1/23/332Mekolichick40-46.pdf

Mertz, N. T. (2004). What's a mentor, anyway? *Educational Administration Quarterly, 40*(4), 541–560.

Mertz, N. T., & Pfleeger, S. L. (2002). Using mentoring to advance females and minorities in a corporate environment. In F. K. Kochan (Ed.), *The organizational and human dimensions of successful mentoring programs and relationships* (pp. 221–242). Greenwich, CT: Information Age.

Meyers, K. L., Sillim, S. E., Ohland, N. L., & Ohland, M. W. (2010). A comparison of engineering students' reflections on their first-year experiences. *Journal of Engineering Education, 99*(2), 169–178.

Michael, A. E., Dickson, J., Ryan, B., & Koefer, A. (2010). College prep blueprint for bridging and scaffolding incoming freshmen: Practices that work. *College Student Journal, 44*(4), 969–978.

Miller, A. (2002). *Mentoring Students and Young People: A Handbook of Effective Practice.* London, England: Kogan Page.

Molm, L. D. (2006). The social exchange framework. In P. J. Burke (Ed.), *Contemporary social psychological theories* (pp. 24–45). Stanford, CA: Stanford Social Sciences.

Murdock, J. L., Stipanovic, N., & Lucas, K. (2013). Fostering connections between graduate students and strengthening professional identity through co-mentoring. *British Journal of Guidance & Counselling, 41*(5), 487–503.

Museus, S. D., & Neville, K. M. (2012). Delineating the ways that key institutional agents provide racial minority students with access to social capital in college. *Journal of College Student Development, 53*(3), 436–452. doi:10.1353/csd.2012.0042

Nora, A., & Crisp, G. (2007). Mentoring students: Conceptualizing and validating the multi-dimensions of a support system. *Journal of College Student Retention: Research, Theory and Practice, 9*(3), 337–356.

Noufou, O., Rezania, D., & Hossain, M. (2014). Measuring and exploring factors affecting students' willingness to engage in peer mentoring. *International Journal of Mentoring and Coaching in Education, 3*(2), 141–157.

O'Brien, M., Llamas, M., & Stevens, E. (2012). Lessons learned from four years of peer mentoring in a tiered group program within education. *Journal of the Australia and New Zealand Student Services Association, 40,* 7–15.

Ochoa, E. O., Lunsford, L. G., Minera, C. E. C., & Fosmire, A. (2015). Seeing the unseen: Lessons from a case study on mentoring underrepresented students in research. *Perspectives on Undergraduate Research and Mentoring, 4*(1). Retrieved from http://blogs.elon.edu/purm/2015/11/16/seeing-the-unseen-lessons-from-a-case-study-on-mentoring-underrepresented-students-in-research/

O'Meara, K., Knudsen, K., & Jones, J. (2013). The role of emotional competencies in faculty-doctoral student relationships. *Review of Higher Education, 36*(3), 315–347.

Owens, D., Lacey, K., Rawls, G., & Holbert-Quince, J. A. (2010). First-generation African American male college students: Implications for career counselors. *Career Development Quarterly, 58*(4), 291–300.

Palmer, R., & Gasman, M. (2008). "It takes a village to raise a child": The role of social capital in promoting academic success for African American men at a Black college. *Journal of College Student Development, 49*(1), 52–70.

Parks-Yancy, R. (2012). Interactions into opportunities: Career management for low-income, first-generation African American college students. *Journal of College Student Development, 53*(4), 510–523.

Pascarella, E. T., & Terenzini P. T. (2005) *How college affects students: A third decade of research.* San Francisco, CA: Jossey-Bass.

Patton, L. D. (2009). My sister's keeper: A qualitative examination of mentoring experiences among African American women in graduate and professional schools. *The Journal of Higher Education, 80*(5), 510–537.

Peer Mentoring. (n.d.). National Collegiate Honors Council. Retrieved from http://nchc honors.org/faculty-directors/peer-mentoring-programs/

Perna, L., Lundy-Wagner, V., Drezner, N. D., Gasman, M., Yoon, S., Bose, E., & Gary, S. (2009). The contribution of HBCUs to the preparation of African American women for STEM careers: A case study. *Research in Higher Education, 50*(1), 1–23.

Phinney, J. S., Campos, T., Cidhinnia, M., Padilla Kallemeyn, D. M., & Kim, C. (2011). Processes and outcomes of a mentoring program for Latino college freshmen. *Journal of Social Issues, 67*(3), 599–621.

Pfund, C., Pribbenow, C. M., Branchaw, J., Lauffer, S. M., & Handelsman, J. (2006). The merits of training mentors. *Science, 311*(5760), 473–474.

Posse Foundation. (n.d.). *We develop tomorrow's leaders.* Retrieved from https://www.posse foundation.org/about-posse

Poteat, L. F., Shockley, K. M., & Allen, T. D. (2009). Mentor-protégé commitment fit and relationship satisfaction in academic mentoring. *Journal of Vocational Behavior*, *74*(3), 332–337.

Ragins, B. R., & McFarlin, D. (1990). Perception of mentor roles in cross-gender mentoring relationships. *Journal of Vocational Behavior*, *37*, 321–339.

Reddick, R. J., & Pritchett, K. O. (2015). "I don't want to work in a world of Whiteness": White faculty and their mentoring relationships with Black students. *Journal of the Professoriate*, *8*(1), 54–84.

Reid, M. J., & Moore, J. L. (2008). College readiness and academic preparation for postsecondary education oral histories of first-generation urban college students. *Urban Education*, *43*(2), 240–261.

Reilly, R. C., & D'Amico, M. (2011). Mentoring undergraduate university women survivors of childhood abuse and intimate partner violence. *Journal of College Student Development*, *52*(4), 409–424. doi:10.1353/csd.2011.0046

Rickinson, B. (1998). The relationship between undergraduate student counselling and successful degree completion. *Studies in Higher Education*, *23*(1), 95–102.

Rios-Aguilar, C., & Deil-Amen, R. (2010). Beyond getting in and fitting in: An examination of social networks and professionally relevant social capital among Latina/o university students. *Journal of Hispanic Higher Education*, *11*(2), 179–196. doi:10.1177/1538192711435555

Rios-Aguilar, C., & Deil-Amen, R. (2012). Beyond getting in and fitting in an examination of social networks and professionally relevant social capital among Latina/o university students. *Journal of Hispanic Higher Education*, *11*(2), 179–196.

Rios-Ellis, B., Rascón, M., Galvez, G., Inzunza-Franco, G., Bellamy, L., & Torres, A. (2015). Creating a model of Latino peer education: Weaving cultural capital into the fabric of academic services in an urban university setting. *Education and Urban Society*, *47*(1), 33–55.

Rusbult, C. E. (1983). A longitudinal test of the Investment Model: The development (and deterioration) of satisfaction and commitment in heterosexual involvements. *Journal of Personality and Social Psychology*, *45*, 101–117.

Russell, S. H., Hancock, M. P., & McCullough, J. (2007). Benefits of undergraduate research experiences. *Science*, *316*(5824), 548–549.

Salinitri, G. (2005). The effects of formal mentoring on the retention rates for first-year, low achieving students. *Canadian Journal of Education/Revue Canadienne de l'education*, *28*(4), 853–873.

Sams, D., Lewis, R., McMullen, R., Bacnik, L., Hammack, J., Richards, R., & Powell, C. (2015). Measuring self-efficacy and scientific literacy across disciplines at value-added outcomes of undergraduate research mentoring: Scale development. *Council on Undergraduate Research Quarterly*, *35*(3), 23–30.

Schreiner, L. A., Noel, P., Anderson, E., & Cantwell, L. (2011). The impact of faculty and staff on high-risk college student persistence. *Journal of College Student Development*, *52*(3), 321–338. doi:10.1353/csd.2011.0044

Schultz, P. W., Hernandez, P. R., Woodcock, A., Estrada, M., Chance, R. C., Aguilar, M., & Serpe, R. T. (2011). Patching the pipeline: Reducing educational disparities in the sciences through minority training programs. *Educational Evaluation and Policy Analysis*, *33*(1), 95–114. doi:10.3102/0162373710392371

Shanahan, J. O., Ackley-Holbrook, E., Hall, E., Stewart, K., & Walkington, H. (2015). Ten salient practices of undergraduate research mentors: A review of the literature. *Mentoring & Tutoring: Partnership in Learning, 23*(5), 359–376. doi:10.1080/13611267.2015.1126162

Shojai, S., Davis, W. J., & Root, P. S. (2014). Developmental relationship programs: An empirical study of the impact of peer-mentoring programs. *Contemporary Issues in Education Research (Online), 7*(1), 31–38.

Shrestha, C. H., May, S., Edirisingha, P., Burke, L., & Linsey, T. (2009). From face-to-face to e-mentoring: Does the "e" add any value for mentors? *International Journal of Teaching and Learning in Higher Education, 20*(2), 116–124.

Slovacek, S. P., Peterfreund, A. R., Kuehn, G. D., Whittinghill, J. C., Tucker, S., Rath, K. A., & Reinke, Y. G. (2011). Minority students severely underrepresented in science, technology engineering and math. *Journal of STEM Education, 12*(1–2), 5–16.

Smojver Ažić, S., & Antulic, S. (2013). Adjustment to college and the student mentoring programme/Prilagodba studiju i programu studentskog mentorstva. *Croatian Journal of Education [Hrvatski časopis za odgoj i obrazovanje], 15*(3), 715–740.

Stanford, D., & Shattell, M. (2010). Using an honors program to engage undergraduate students in research. *Nursing Education Perspectives, 31*(5), 325–326.

Straus, S. E., Johnson, M. O., Marquez, C., & Feldman, M. D. (2013). Characteristics of successful and failed mentoring relationships: A qualitative study across two academic health centers. *Academic Medicine, 88*(1), 82–89.

Tentoni, S. C. (1995). The mentoring of counseling students: A concept in search of a paradigm. *Counselor Education and Supervision, 35*(1), 32–42.

Terrion, J. L., & Leonard, D. (2007). A taxonomy of the characteristics of student peer mentors in higher education: Findings from a literature review. *Mentoring & Tutoring: Partnership in Learning, 15*(2), 149–164.

Thiry, H., Laursen, S. L., & Hunter, A. B. (2011). What experiences help students become scientists? A complete study of research and other sources of personal and professional gains for STEM undergraduates. *Journal of Higher Education, 82*(4), 357–388. doi:10.1353/jhe.2011.0023

Thompson, L., Jefferies, M., & Topping, K. (2010). E-mentoring for e-learning development. *Innovations in Education and Teaching International, 47*(3), 305–315.

Tierney, W. G., & Bensimon, E. M. (1996). *Promotion and tenure: Community and socialization in academe.* Albany, NY: SUNY Press.

Tinto, V. (1993). *Leaving college: Rethinking causes and cures of student attrition* (2nd ed.). Chicago, IL: University of Chicago Press.

Torres Campos, C. M., Phinney, J. S., Perez-Brena, N., Kim, C., Ornelas, B., Nemanim, L., ...Ramirez, C. (2009). A mentor-based targeted intervention for high-risk Latino college freshmen: A pilot study. *Journal of Hispanic Higher Education, 8*(2), 158–178. doi:10.1177/1538192708317621">/1538192708317621

Tovar, E. (2014). The role of faculty, counselors, and support programs on Latino/a community college students' success and intent to persist. *Community College Review.* Advance online publication. doi:0091552114553788

Van Vliet, K. J., Klingle, K. E., & Hiseler, L. E. (2013). The mentorship of undergraduate students in counselling psychology research. *Counselling Psychology Quarterly, 26*(3–4), 406–426.

von der Borch, P., Stormann, D. S., Meinel, F. G., Moder, S., Reincke, M., Tekian, A., & Fischer, M. R. (2011). A novel large-scale mentoring program for medical students based on a quantitative and qualitative needs analysis. *GMS Zeitschrift fuür Medizinische Ausbildung, 28*(2), 1–16.

Ward, C., Jones, K. W., Coles, R., Rich, L., Knapp, S., & Madsen, R. (2014). Mentored research in a Tribal college setting: The Northern Cheyenne Case. *Journal of Research in Rural Education, 29*(3), 1–17.

Weidman, J. C. (1989). Undergraduate socialization: A conceptual approach. In J. C. Smart (Ed.), *Higher education: Handbook of theory and research* (Vol. 5, pp. 289–322). New York, NY: Agathon Press.

Weidman, J. C. (2006). Socialization of students in higher education. In C. F. Conrad & R. C. Serlin (Eds.), *The Sage handbook for research in education* (pp. 253–262). Thousand Oaks, CA: Sage.

Weidman, J. C., & Stein, E. L. (2003). Socialization of doctoral students to academic norms. *Research in Higher Education, 44*(6), 641–656.

Wisker, G. (2012). *The Good Supervisor: Supervising Postgradaute and Undergraduate Research for Doctoral Theses and Dissertations.* 2nd Ed. Palgrave.

Wilson, Z. S., Holmes, L., deGravelles, K., L., Sylvain, M. R., Batiste, L., Johnson, M., ... Warner, I. M. (2012). Hierarchical mentoring: A transformative strategy for improving diversity and retention in undergraduate STEM disciplines. *Journal of Science Education and Technology, 21*(1), 148–156.

Yosso, T. J. (2005). Whose culture has capital? A critical race theory discussion of community cultural wealth. *Race, Ethnicity, and Education, 8*(1), 69–91.

Zachary, L. J. (2002). The role of teacher as mentor. In J. M. Ross-Gordon (Ed.), *Contemporary Viewpoints on Teaching Adults Effectively*, New Directions for Adult and Continuing Education, *93*, pp. 27–38.

Zell, M. C. (2009). Achieving a college education: The psychological experiences of Latina/o community college students. *Journal of Hispanic Higher Education, 9*(2), 167–186. doi:10.1177/1538192709343102

Zevallos, A. L., & Washburn, M. (2014). Creating a culture of student success: The SEEK scholars peer mentoring program. *About Campus, 18*(6), 25–29.

Name Index

A

Ackley-Holbrook, E., 88
Aguilar, M., 42, 52, 55
Allen, T. D., 23, 88
Alvarado, A. R., 40
Amaral, K. E., 38, 74
Anderson, E., 42
Anderson, E. M., 60
Anderson, M., 53
Antulic, S., 16, 78
Apprey, M., 33, 34, 59, 68, 77
Arment, A., 39, 52, 77
Arment, A. R., 41, 52
Arredondo, P., 41, 42
Astin, A.W., 32, 58, 68, 85
Azic, S. S., 78

B

Bacnik, L., 32, 33
Baker, R., 32, 33, 42
Baker, V. L., 15, 19, 22, 24, 25, 32, 56, 84, 86, 88
Barnett, E. A., 31, 42, 43, 68
Bassett, K. C., 33, 34, 59, 68, 77
Batiste, L., 49, 50
Bean, J., 46
Bearman, S., 55
Beckman, M., 53
Behar-Horenstein, L. S., 17, 38, 76
Bell, A., 33, 44, 86
Bellamy, L., 49
Benishek, L. A., 67, 79, 87

Bensimon, E. M., 80
Berdan, J., 40
Bernard, E., 47
Berwise, C. A., 38, 76, 89
Best, G., 38
Bettinger, E., 32, 33, 42
Bhattacharya, G., 16, 24
Bieschke, K. J., 67
Blackwell, J. E., 18
Bonnett, S., 34, 36
Bordes-Edgar, V., 41, 42
Bose, E., 17, 75
Bourdieu, P., 32, 69, 85
Bower, G. G., 34, 36
Bowman, S. R., 66
Bragg, A. K., 69, 85, 86
Branchaw, J., 88
Branscombe, N. R., 66
Bravo, A., 42
Bridgeland, J., 14
Brittian, A. S., 16
Brown, L. J., 53, 78
Bruce, M., 14
Bruland, H., 35, 77
Budny, D., 51
Burke, L., 39
Burton, L. J., 78

C

Cabrera, N. L., 46, 56
Cambridge-Williams, T., 47
Campbell, C. M., 32, 41, 74

Campos, T., 17
Cantwell, L., 42
Carter, F. D., 48
Chance, R. C., 42, 52, 55
Chang, M. J., 80
Chemers, M. M., 55
Chester, A., 78
Chou, P., 43, 59
Chuateco, L. I., 26
Cidhinnia, M., 17
Coco, K., 39
Cole, D., 17, 24
Coles, R., 34, 87
Collings, R., 14, 40, 50, 68
Connelly, P., 33, 41
Corso, J., 32, 77
Cotton, S. R., 80
Cox, B. E., 80
Cox, C. B., 35, 88
Craney, C., 19, 55, 68, 77
Crisp, G., 15, 18, 19, 21, 27, 28, 29, 31, 32, 33, 35, 37, 42, 43, 44, 61, 73, 75, 84, 87
Crowe, H. A., 33
Cruz, I., 15, 18, 19, 21, 27, 28, 29, 31, 35, 37, 44, 61, 73, 75
Cyrenne, D., 35

D

D'Abate, C. P., 36
Dahlvig, J., 14, 16, 39
D'Amico, M., 36
Daver, Z. E., 47
Davis, D. J., 53
Davis, W. J., 50
Dawson, P., 76
DeAngelo, L., 40
Deaton, B., 77
Deaton, C. C., 77
de Brey, C., 16
DeFreitas, S. C., 42
deGravelles, K., L., 49, 50
Deil-Amen, R., 17, 69, 70
Dennis, J. M., 26
Deschenes, C., 35
Devine, J., 32, 77

Dicke-Bohmann, A. K., 35, 88
Dickson, J., 17, 46
Dix, A. C., 17, 38, 76
Dodson, J. E., 53, 78
Dolan, E., 38, 56
Drezner, N. D., 17, 75
Duff, A., 33, 41
Dugan, J. P., 32, 41, 59, 74
Dunlop, A., 33, 41
Dunlop Velez, E., 16
Dunstan, S. B., 17

E

Eagan, M. K., 46, 56
Eagan, M. K. Jr., 80
Eaton, S. B., 46
Edgcomb, M. R., 33
Edirisingha, P., 39
Elgar, K., 78
Emerson, R. M., 65
Ensher, E. A., 66
Espinoza, A., 17
Espinoza, C. C., 16
Espinoza, P. P., 16
Estrada, M., 42, 52, 55
Evans, S. D., 48

F

Fechheimer, M., 55
Feldman, M. D., 88
Fischer, M. R, 32
Fosmire, A., 55
Fox, A., 33, 41
Fuentes, M. V., 40

G

Galvez, G., 49
Garceau, O., 35
Gary, S., 17, 75
Gasman, M., 17, 75
Gershenfeld, S., 29
Gibb, S., 66
Gibbs, M. K., 37, 44, 82, 88
Girves, J. E., 65, 67, 86
Goff, L., 19
Goza, B. K., 55

Greer, J., 56
Griffin, K. A., 19, 22, 24, 31, 32, 33, 34,
  36, 66, 74, 80, 84, 86, 87, 88
Gross, D., 16, 59
Guay, F., 35
Guiffrida, D. A., 66, 87
Guillory, R. M., 32, 76
Gwathmey, J. K., 65, 67, 86

H

Haddock, S., 16, 33, 74
Hall, E., 88
Hammack, J., 32, 33
Hancock, M. P., 55
Handelsman, J., 88
Harvey, M., 35
Hébert, T. P., 55
Henry, J., 35, 77
Hensel, N., 53
Hernandez, P. R., 42, 52, 55
Higgins, M. C., 62, 79
Hiseler, L. E., 55
Holbert-Quince, J. A., 17
Holland, J. M., 40, 51
Holmes, L., 49, 50
Holt, L. J., 38, 76, 89
Homans, G. C., 66
Hossain, M., 59
Hryciw, D. H., 38
Hunt, D. M., 63, 70, 71, 82
Hunter, A. B., 37, 41, 55
Hurtado, S., 46, 56, 80
Hu, S., 33, 37, 42, 44
Hussar, W., 16

I

Ihas, D., 56
Inkelas, K. K., 47
Inzunza-Franco, G., 49
Ishiyama, J., 61
Iverson, E., 16, 59

J

Jacobi, M., 14, 15, 18, 19, 21, 27, 58, 60,
  67
Jaeger, A. J., 17

Jamookeeah, D., 39
Jefferies, M., 78
Johnson, B. J., 58, 65, 79, 83
Johnson, C. S., 18
Johnson, D., 38, 56
Johnson, M., 49, 50
Johnson, M. O., 88
Johnson, W. B., 18, 64, 80, 83, 84
Jokelainen, M., 39
Jones, J., 88
Jones, K. W., 34, 87

K

Keller, T. E., 65, 79, 82
Kena, G., 16
Kendricks, K., 39, 52, 77
Kendricks, K. D., 41, 52
Ketola, J., 32, 75
Khazanov, L., 14, 33, 42
Kift, S., 47
Kim, C., 17, 40, 75, 78
Kim, Y. K., 24
Kinkel, D. H., 16, 33, 41
Kinzie, J., 24, 26
Kite, M. E., 66
Kitsantas, A., 47
Kleiber, P. B., 55
Klingle, K. E., 55
Knapp, S., 34, 87
Knudsen, K., 88
Koefer, A., 17, 46
Komarraju, M., 16, 24
Komives, S. R., 32, 41, 59, 74
Kostovich, C. T., 39, 43
Krafchick, J., 16, 33, 74
Kram, K., 18, 21, 84
Kram, K. E., 21, 32, 60, 61, 62, 63, 79,
  80, 84, 88
Kuehn, G. D., 15, 39
Kuh, G. D., 24, 26
Kurpius, S. R., 41, 42

L

Lacey, K., 17
Larose, S., 35, 64, 80
Lauffer, S. M., 88

Subject Index

A
Academic advisor, 24
Academic progress and success, 41–42

B
Black Colleges and Universities, 82

C
College adjustment and development, 40–41
College Student Mentoring Scale (CSMS), 35
Council on Undergraduate Research, 52
Critical Race Theory, 70
Cultural capital, 17

F
Faculty members, role of, 24–25. *See also* Mentoring

G
The Good Supervisor, 24
Grade point averages (GPA), 16
Graduate students, role of, 25–26. *See also* Mentoring
Group mentoring, role of, 20. *See also* Mentoring

H
Hispanic Serving Institution (HSI), 42, 49
Homophily, 66

I
International Mentoring Association, 74

M
Mentor; peer, 38; Role index, 61; role of, 36
Mentoring; benefits, 38–40; definitions and characteristics of, 18–23; future research, 75–81; importance and value of, 16–18; limitations of, 28; literature analysis, 26–28; perceptions, functions and roles of, 35–38; practices, evidence-based, 86–89; sensemaking and expectations, 33–35; undergraduate students, 81–86
The Mentoring Effect, 14
Mentoring theories and frameworks, 59; outcomes-based frameworks, 67–71; process-based frameworks, 62–67; typology-related frameworks, 59–62
Meyerhoff Scholarship Program, 48
Monograph, purpose of, 29–30
Multicultural Feminist model, 67

N
National Collegiate Honors Council, 50
National Institutes of Health (NIH), 42
National Science Foundation Research Experiences for Undergraduates, 52
New Student Services Orientation, 46

About the Authors

Gloria Crisp is an associate professor at Oregon State University and co-editor of *New Directions for Institutional Research*. Her scholarship explores the impact of mentoring and other experiences that support students' success at 2- and 4-year accessible institutions. Gloria has contributed to over 40 publications including serving as co-editor for a recent special issue of *New Directions for Community Colleges* (NDCC) focused on student success programming. Her survey instrument, the College Student Mentoring Scale (CSMS), is currently being used at institutions across the country and abroad to evaluate the effectiveness of mentoring relationships. Gloria's research has been supported by the National Science Foundation (NSF), the Association for Institutional Research (AIR), and the Hispanic Association of Colleges and Universities (HACU).

Vicki L. Baker is a professor of economics and management at Albion College in Albion, Michigan and an instructor of business administration for the World Campus at the Pennsylvania State University. She has published 50 articles, chapters, essays, and monographs on the topics of identity development, mentoring, and the faculty experience, with a particular focus on liberal arts colleges. Her research focuses on the role of developmental relationships, at the student and faculty levels, on personal and professional identity development. Her past work has included an examination of the various relationships that support undergraduate students as well as the factors that contribute to fit between a mentor and protégé. Vicki is principal investigator of a study of faculty development in liberal arts colleges, in which mentoring and other sources of support for faculty is a key consideration. She recently served as a Mentoring Undergraduate Research Fellow through Elon University's Center for Engaged Learning. Vicki is the co-founder of Lead Mentor Develop, LLC (www.leadmentordevelop.com).

Kimberly A. Griffin is an associate professor in the College of Education at the University of Maryland in the Counseling, Higher Education, and Special Education Department. The focus of her research is access and equity in higher education, and includes an emphasis on mentoring, career development, and developmental relationships at critical time-points. She has engaged in research addressing the experiences, motivation, and outcomes of Black professors who mentor, definitions of mentoring and other developmental relationships, and the impact of faculty relationships on science identity and career development in graduate training. Kimberly is co-principal investigator on a project examining the nature and influence of mentoring in STEM graduate programs, with an emphasis on students of color.

Laura G. Lunsford studies the psychology of mentoring and leader development. She has published over 30 articles, case studies and chapters on leadership, mentorship dysfunction, optimizing mentoring relationships, and evaluating mentoring. The Department of Education, National Science Foundation, and the Institute for Education Sciences have funded her work on mentoring. She is a co-editor of the SAGE *Handbook of Mentoring* and authored the *Mentoring Handbook for Program Managers* published by Routledge. Lunsford was a tenured associate professor at the University of Arizona before becoming the director of the Swain Center at the Cameron School of Business, University of North Carolina Wilmington. She received the 2009 International Mentoring Association's Dissertation Award for her work on doctoral student mentoring and advising. Laura is the co-founder of Lead Mentor Develop, LLC (www.leadmentordevelop.com).

Meghan J. Pifer is an associate professor of higher education and senior assistant director of the Cadre and Faculty Development Program at the University of Louisville. She studies colleges and universities as organizational contexts. She is interested in understanding the ways in which identity and individual characteristics, and interpersonal networks and relationships, within those contexts shape both individual and organizational outcomes. Her prior research includes consideration of the mentoring experiences of underrepresented students in geosciences, doctoral students across disciplines and identity characteristics, and faculty members at various career stages. She is currently co-principal investigator in a collaborative research study of faculty members' professional experiences and mentoring needs within liberal arts colleges.

About the ASHE Higher Education Report Series

Since 1983, the ASHE (formerly ASHE-ERIC) Higher Education Report Series has been providing researchers, scholars, and practitioners with timely and substantive information on the critical issues facing higher education. Each monograph presents a definitive analysis of a higher education problem or issue, based on a thorough synthesis of significant literature and institutional experiences. Topics range from planning to diversity and multiculturalism, to performance indicators, to curricular innovations. The mission of the Series is to link the best of higher education research and practice to inform decision making and policy. The reports connect conventional wisdom with research and are designed to help busy individuals keep up with the higher education literature. Authors are scholars and practitioners in the academic community. Each report includes an executive summary, review of the pertinent literature, descriptions of effective educational practices, and a summary of key issues to keep in mind to improve educational policies and practice.

This series is one of the most peer reviewed in higher education. A National Advisory Board made up of ASHE members reviews proposals. A National Review Board of ASHE scholars and practitioners reviews completed manuscripts. Six monographs are published each year, and they are approximately 144 pages in length. The reports are widely disseminated through Jossey-Bass and John Wiley & Sons, and they are available online to subscribing institutions through Wiley Online Library (http://wileyonlinelibrary.com).

Call for Proposals

The ASHE Higher Education Report Series is actively looking for proposals. We encourage you to contact one of the editors, Dr. Kelly Ward (kaward@wsu.edu) or Dr. Lisa Wolf-Wendel (lwolf@ku.edu), with your ideas.

ASHE HIGHER EDUCATION REPORT

ORDER FORM SUBSCRIPTION AND SINGLE ISSUES

DISCOUNTED BACK ISSUES:

Use this form to receive 20% off all back issues of *ASHE Higher Education Report.*
All single issues priced at **$23.20** (normally $29.00)

TITLE   ISSUE NO.   ISBN

_____   _____   _____
_____   _____   _____
_____   _____   _____

Call 1-800-835-6770 or see mailing instructions below. When calling, mention the promotional code JBNND to receive your discount. For a complete list of issues, please visit www.wiley.com/WileyCDA/WileyTitle/productCd-AEHE.html

SUBSCRIPTIONS: (1 YEAR, 6 ISSUES)

☐ New Order   ☐ Renewal

U.S.	☐ Individual: $174	☐ Institutional: $347
CANADA/MEXICO	☐ Individual: $174	☐ Institutional: $437
ALL OTHERS	☐ Individual: $210	☐ Institutional: $491

Call 1-800-835-6770 or see mailing and pricing instructions below.
Online subscriptions are available at www.onlinelibrary.wiley.com

ORDER TOTALS:

Issue / Subscription Amount: $ _____

Shipping Amount: $ _____
(for single issues only – subscription prices include shipping)

Total Amount: $ _____

SHIPPING CHARGES:

First Item	$6.00
Each Add'l Item	$2.00

(No sales tax for U.S. subscriptions. Canadian residents, add GST for subscription orders. Individual rate subscriptions must be paid by personal check or credit card. Individual rate subscriptions may not be resold as library copies.)

BILLING & SHIPPING INFORMATION:

☐ **PAYMENT ENCLOSED:** *(U.S. check or money order only. All payments must be in U.S. dollars.)*

☐ **CREDIT CARD:**   ☐ VISA   ☐ MC   ☐ AMEX

Card number _____Exp. Date_____

Card Holder Name_____Card Issue # _____

Signature _____Day Phone_____

☐ **BILL ME:** *(U.S. institutional orders only. Purchase order required.)*

Purchase order # _____
Federal Tax ID 13559302 • GST 89102-8052

Name_____

Address_____

Phone_____ E-mail_____

Copy or detach page and send to: **John Wiley & Sons, Inc. / Jossey Bass**
PO Box 55381
Boston, MA 02205-9850

PROMO JBNND